MITCH MURRAY'S

ONE-LINERS

FOR

BUSINESS

**and how to use them
in your speech**

MITCH MURRAY'S ONE-LINERS

FOR

BUSINESS

and how to use them in your speech

foulsham
LONDON • NEW YORK • TORONTO • SYDNEY

foulsham

The Publishing House, Bennetts Close,
Cippenham, Slough, Berkshire, SL1 5AP, England.

Other books by the same author:

Mitch Murray's One-Liners for Weddings
Mitch Murray's One-Liners for Speeches on Special Occasions

both published by Foulsham

ISBN: 0-572-02495-9

Edited by Carole Chapman
Printed in Great Britain by St Edmundsbury Press Ltd, Bury St Edmunds,
Suffolk.

CONTENTS

WELCOME TO ONE-LINER LAND

Names and characters in this book are used solely for the purpose of example. Any similarity between these fictional illustrations and real people is entirely coincidental.

So put that lawyer away and don't be silly!

INTRODUCTION

You've been asked to make a speech . . . or a sales pitch . . . or a presentation.

The substance of what you have to say is clear: 'welcome', 'well-done', 'buy from us', 'happy retirement' . . . whatever.

That's not the problem . . .

What you really need are little quips, bits of colour, tension-breakers, wake-up calls. In other words – one-liners.

Well cowboy, you're in luck. Here comes the cavalry!

INTRODUCTION

Chapter One

THE IMPORTANCE OF NOT BEING EARNEST

If you're a young executive trying to climb the corporate ladder but discovering that, in truth, it's a greasy pole, this book will help you.

There is no better showcase for an individual in business than the one provided by the opportunity of speaking in public. They have no choice but to notice you. All *you* have to do is grab and hold their attention.

I realise that for many people, the looming prospect of having to stand up and speak to an audience is terrifying to contemplate. Yet, it really is a golden opportunity to super-charge your career.

Let's assume you have the potential to make it. How do you get this across to the powers-that-be? You simply can't go through your working day blatantly flagging your talents.

Too obvious.

Ability itself is not enough.

People have to see you in action. They have to concentrate on what you're saying and be made to realise that you know what you're talking about. Using one-liners, selectively, will help remove that air of intensity and desperation which – believe me – is very off-putting in young 'wannabe' execs.

Don't forget, the old geezer who promotes you is probably going to have to work closely with you. He wants someone he can relax with, someone who can cover for him, someone who doesn't scare him.

Take heart . . . the fact that you bought this book and have read as far as this, proves that you're thinking in the right way. You've realised that almost any speech or presentation will benefit greatly from the occasional quip or one-liner, provided the humour is entirely in character with the person making the speech and appropriate to the audience.

Did you *realise* you realised that?

These little sound-splashes bring a sense of proportion to issues, help the audience to concentrate on the subject and enhance the general charisma of the speaker.

You know, when it comes to old proverbs, I'm a bit of a revisionist. Some of these sayings are *dangerously* wrong. For instance:

'The way to a man's heart is through his stomach.'

Try telling *that* to the Royal College of Surgeons!

'Love Thy Neighbour.'

Oh yeah? Have you seen the size of her old man?!

'If at first you don't succeed, try, try, try again.'

Unless you're playing Russian Roulette.

Ordinarily at this point, I'd rest my case, but I just remembered that I'm meant to be developing an argument, so in the spirit of my revisionism, I now present to you:

'*Words* speak louder than *actions*.'

Think about it.

Consider the illusion created by the foreigner who speaks fluent English. He gives us the impression that he's highly intelligent. He may be as dumb as they come, his excellent use of our language could be the only skill he has, yet we see him as very bright.

On what basis do we vote for politicians?

If they are – as yet – unproven, we listen to their words. It's the only way we can assess their potential. Of course, once in office the guy may have an aptitude only for ineptitude, but by then, it's too late.

We've bought the Skoda.

He or she – through effective communication – managed to create the illusion of competence.

Adolf Hitler's passionate rhetoric inspired the confidence of the German people, who didn't find out until later that he was a destructive politician, a lousy commander-in-chief and useless at needlepoint.

So, whether you're selling a product, a concept, or your ability to do a more important job, you've been given a hearing.

Don't waste it.

Allow me to help you inject a bit of magic into your one-man-show.

Chapter Two

HOW TO USE THIS BOOK

I think I can guess the rough sequence of events which led you to this page; you wandered into the bookshop, browsed through the various sections and happened upon this mini-masterpiece.

Having decided it didn't need much reading, you bought it.

I can understand that.

I realise that you people in business are very busy, what with lunches, cocktail receptions, golf tournaments . . . Who wants to start wading through a text book packed with intricate training techniques in the art of presentation and creativity? We're all too busy for that kind of crap.

At the risk of sounding Forrest Gumpish, this book is like a box of chocolates: you really don't have to go through it systematically, just pick at what you fancy.

After all, you've paid for it.

Please feel free to go prospecting for those glittering little sequins you'll be embroidering into your speech. Then, when you're in the right frame of mind, check out some of my sneaky tricks of the trade and take an occasional glance at some of the instructional stuff.

No need to read this book cover-to-cover. I won't be offended. I'm only in this for the money, you know.

I'll offer you advice on style and delivery, and we'll look at the options of whether you should learn your speech or read it.

Of course, when it comes to the content of your pitch, your report, your business analysis . . . you're on your own. I can't give you powers of persuasion, common sense, clarity of vision or knowledge of your own industry. I have to assume that as you were smart enough to buy this book, you already have these qualities in abundance.

But what I *can* do is show you how to use humour as a tool. At times, warn you against its excesses. At other times, encourage you to be bold.

Taken together, these guidelines will go a long way towards tackling the paradox which faces most public speakers at one time or another and which, very soon, may well be facing you. Namely, how can you hope to instil confidence in your audience when you yourself are in imminent danger of a serious laundry problem?!

Chapter Three

TIMING AND STYLE

A good speech, like a good song, needs a regular beat.

It should have a rhythm of its own: peaks, troughs, crescendos and a climax. (Don't you love it when I talk dirty?)

Think about the character of your speech. Is it a ballad, or is it rock and roll?

Consider these factors:
- What time of the day is it?
- What's the size and composition of your audience?
- What's the nature of your message?

If you're trying to put across a thoughtful analysis of your corporate strategy in front of twenty-six regional managers, the pace of your presentation will be quite different from a rousing end-of-conference 'go get 'em' blockbuster.

Choose and construct your material according to the circumstances, and the rhythm of that speech – along with its highs and lows – will happen almost automatically.

Your form of delivery, the style of material and the amount of material you use will, to a great extent, depend on the clock.

EARLY MORNING?

Their funny bones are still asleep. Keep it simple and businesslike; morning humour should be restricted to the occasional quip or witty comment. Nothing too subtle. Nothing too long. Nothing contrived.

AFTER LUNCH?

Give it some welly! They're ready for it. They've eaten, they've sipped a little wine, they've chatted. They're warmed up.

Warning: Don't overdo it. The day's still young and there's too much work ahead to be flippant.

AFTER DINNER?

The traditional time for brandy, cigars and laughter. People are receptive to a little entertainment immediately after the meal. They're laid-back, mellow, relaxed . . . Okay, let's face it – they're pissed!

If you have any say in the programme, don't leave it too

long before you speak or your audience will start to become impatient or unruly or over-tired or aggressive . . . or any combination of the above.

If this happens, you'll have to revert to your early morning approach and cut the speech by two-thirds.

(I'm ever so pleased *I* won't be there.)

Don't try to be too businesslike when your speech is made in the after-dinner slot; at that time, the atmosphere is one of informality, and too much emphasis on company matters won't go down very well. Treat your after-dinner talk as a pseudo-social speech and construct it accordingly.

Well of *course* I'm going to help you construct it.

Sort of.

Chapter Four

STARTING TO WRITE

Many professional writers have adopted a simple little system for making speeches sound really significant.

You may like to try it yourself. Just think of something really stupid to say, and then write the opposite.

I'm not being much help, am I? Let's start again.

Speechmaking – whether social, political or corporate – can only ever be an exercise in superficiality. It simply isn't a medium which allows you unlimited expansion and embellishment of your thoughts. Give a speech too much substance and it becomes a lecture.

Think about it. You usually have a few short minutes to get your points across, during which, hopefully, your audience will be glued to their seats. (Come to think of it, with the right glue, it could work!)

Nowadays, the average audience has the attention span of a stick of broccoli.

To be memorable, your speech needs bullet points, catchy words and humour.

No matter how important the subject, you have to resist the temptation to expand every argument, examine every area and explore every avenue. Don't go in for the kind of detail the Prosecution pursued in the OJ Simpson trial or *your* jury will kick you up the bum as well.

Nowadays, people are programmed to absorb soundbites. These spoken headlines have to be linked together with little verbal bridges and will need to follow a logical path.

You'll see what I'm getting at later in the book, once you've looked at some examples.

With this technique, however, one word in the wrong place and you've blown the joke. So a little farther on, I'll be showing you how to minimise that risk.

Don't worry, I won't forget. I've made a note of it.

If you need help with a forthcoming presentation on a purely business-related subject, you've probably started injecting material from this book already.

When it comes to putting together speeches of that kind, you almost certainly know best and all you really want from this book are a few good comedy ideas.

Fine.

I'm going to be concentrating on writing techniques for the construction of the social-style business speech I mentioned earlier.

Let me start by recommending that your speech is a cleverly crafted succession of strong one-liners in a natural, flowing format.

That's it.

No long jokes, no anecdotes, no stories . . . just one-liners.

(I should point out that I'm using the term 'one-liners' in a very generalised way; sometimes you'll be using two- or three-line gags, sometimes the one-liner won't be a funny line at all – it could be a sentimental comment or piece of prose.)

In my opinion, the one-liner construction is ideal for most after-dinner speeches; the rhythm is simple to maintain, your investment shows a return every seven or eight seconds and the format creates the illusion of a shorter, snappier speech – very handy if you're not exactly an experienced orator.

If a joke or a comment falls flat . . . so what? You're straight into the next line and, chances are, nobody will even notice that your one-liner didn't work.

On the other hand, the longer story or anecdote is an investment which has to pay off. If a thirty-second story dies a death, you have a real problem! We've all suffered the bloke who genuinely thinks he's a raconteur but in reality couldn't tell the difference between a comma and a coma!

There are occasions, however, when an incident or an amusing episode is so well known that you will be expected to make some mention of it. Don't repeat the whole story (unless your name is Peter Ustinov). As an experience, it may have been funny if you were there at the time, but as part of an otherwise fast-moving speech, you risk losing your audience.

The trick is merely to *allude* to the event by using an appropriate one-liner. For instance, let's assume it's common knowledge that Andy, one of your team with a reputation for fast and scary driving, recently managed to spin his Audi off the road.

No need to relate the whole incident. One gag will do the job:

> **You may have noticed Andy Wilson's car parked outside . . .**
> **It's a very unusual vehicle . . . it has four headlights, two radiators, and the engine's in the back.**
>
> **Of course it wasn't always like that . . . only since the accident.**

If your chief planning officer tripped and tumbled down the steps of the Town Hall, you only have to remind people of . . .

> **The day Richard Cowley re-discovered gravity.**

Get the picture?

As you glance through the one-liners in this book, you may find that many of them need to be read aloud in order for you to see the joke.

This illustrates how important it is to remember that you are writing for the *ear*, not for the eye.

Your audience will be listening, not reading.

Your wording must sound natural. Don't say 'she is' when you'd normally say 'she's'. Don't say 'I am' when you'd normally say 'I'm'. Don't say 'you will', say 'you'll' – unless, of course, you're deliberately emphasising the word 'will' as in 'You *will* tell your friends about this book, won't you?'

Use normal language, not pseudo 'speech-talk'.

As my mother once advised her friend Celia, who was about to make an important speech, 'Don't try to be clever – just be yourself'.

Chapter Five

EDITING, PADDING AND LINKING

The one-liner format also means easy editing on-site. Suppose someone you intended to welcome hasn't turned up. Simply skip that part of the speech and carry on with the next segment.

If, despite your personality and witty presentation, you begin to sense that the audience has had enough, it's an easy matter to cut from where you are to a later section, or even straight to the close of the speech. See my section on 'Closings', and I'll show you how to get away with it.

With our one-liner construction, the omissions shouldn't affect the flow. Most of the lines are self-contained. If you're doing two or three one-liners about your Scottish office supervisor's healthy ego, just use the best one. Make sure, however, that your link words are suitable and are not too repetitive.

So now you're thinking, 'What the hell are 'link words'?'

Right?

You see, I knew *exactly* what you were thinking. We authors are very clever people.

'Link words' are what I call the little spoken punctuations and phrases used to move from one line or topic to another; words like 'Now . . .', 'Nevertheless . . .', 'You know . . .', 'Mind you . . .', 'After all . . .', 'In any case . . .'

Simply reciting pages of one-liners without the use of link words wouldn't work in a speech. You need them in order to bond your lines together, thereby creating the illusion of a natural progression.

Don't forget, you're coming out of a laugh into the next gag, and it's more impressive for the audience to feel their laughter has forced you to pause than for you to appear as if you're throwing lines at them and hoping for the best.

You also need to 'bridge' from one subject to another in order to maintain a logical flow.

You should never be able to see the join.

In the following example, I'll be making several points about my victim, I'll be using 'link words' (underlined), and I'll be 'bridging' from subject to subject straight into the closing of my speech.

All this while drinking a glass of water.

What a man!

The 'victim' is Stuart Reid – a timber merchant. He's decided to take 'Late Retirement' and this speech is being made at his farewell party. We cover his pathetic attempts at keeping

fit, his enthusiasm for alcohol, his admiration for the opposite sex, his shaky medical profile and – the dominant theme – his advanced years.
Poor sod.

We join the speech three quarters of the way through.

. . . by the way, I happen to know that last month, Stuart went out and bought eight men's health magazines, six general fitness publications, four manuals on exercise and a medical encyclopedia . . . They had an influence on his health all right . . . while he was carrying them out to the garage, he ruptured himself!

Nevertheless, he still takes fitness quite seriously. At home, he even has his own parallel bars . . .

One for brandy, one for scotch!

Okay, so Stuart Reid enjoys a drink . . . what's wrong with that?

To be fair, he's cut down quite a bit. This guy used to drink so much gin, Gordon's thought he was a wholesaler!

. . . but recently, one of his many lady friends told him he was like a load of fireworks in November . . . bloody useless after the fifth!

Funnily enough, it's just been announced that, to coincide with Stuart's retirement, they're going to be hanging his zip in the Timber Merchant's Hall of Fame.

Oh yes, Stuart was always quite a ladies man.

Mind you, the only hot number he's into these days is his blood pressure!

There was a time, when he was younger, he'd do anything to go out with a nurse . . .
Nowadays, of course, he daren't go out with*out* a nurse!

Never mind Stuart, there's good news . . . according to current medical opinion, there's no reason you shouldn't be able to enjoy sex past ninety . . .

. . . as long as you let somebody else drive!

Ladies and gentlemen, despite his age, Stuart Reid has quite a lot going . . .
his hair's going, his teeth are going, his liver's going . . .
Come to think of it, *I'd* better be going! I've only got three minutes left and I usually need that for applause . . . so please join me in drinking a toast to . . .'

So now you know how to use link words, not only for the purpose of joining lines together in a natural way, but also to keep your audience alert.

At times, it sounds as if you are defending the victim. However, this 'defence' is merely a device which gives you the excuse to continue laying into him.

I call it 'Safe Slander', and you'll find more on this in the section on 'Roasts and Insults'.

And don't worry . . . your victim will love it!

I think.

NOTE

In the various one-liners listed in this book, most of those suitable for bridging from one subject to the next will be specially indicated. The subsequent subject will usually be quite obvious. With a little imagination, however, you'll be able to bridge from many others.

Chapter Six

ORIGINALITY

What makes this book rather unusual is that a very high proportion of the material on offer is totally original. I am not primarily an editor, merely collecting and compiling existing quotes and old chestnuts, I am, first and foremost, a writer.

Of course you'll find plenty of familiar one-liners too – some of them are so useful, I would have been doing you a disservice to have ignored them. However, I have usually freshened these up or adapted them in order to make them more effective for use in business speeches.

The truly original lines are easy to spot:
anything funny you've never heard before is mine.

Believe me, I don't need to nick anything.

When I do, it's for the pure joy of larceny.

As you make more and more speeches, you're going to find yourself researching other joke books, comedy publications and dictionaries of humorous quotations.

You get extra points with an audience if your material is, or sounds, original. If you personalise your one-liners accurately enough, you may well create that illusion.

You also get extra points for topicality. What's the big news story on the day of your speech? Can you adapt a line cleverly enough to refer to it?

No?

Oh.

Tough!

If you find yourself having to steal, at least do it sensibly. Try to use totally original gags; it doesn't matter where you pinch them from. After all, the line between 'inspired by' and 'nicked from' is a very fine one.

Don't just pick up any old gag; you don't know where it's been.

Don't use a joke Jimmy Tarbuck told the previous night on network television . . . half the country would have heard it.

NOTE

One who steals someone else's creative work is known as a plagiarist. The word 'plagiarism' is derived from the Latin, 'plagium', meaning 'kidnapping'.

By the way, I copied that sentence out of somebody else's book!

If you're addressing an industry of which you have no intimate experience, be careful. For instance, you're Guest of Honour at the Hospitality Inn Hotel Group's Annual Gala Dinner, and you say:

> **. . . earlier this evening, I was delighted to hear your chairman announcing this year's greatly improved results.**
> **I'd like to take this opportunity of congratulating you all. It seems like only yesterday things were so bad in the hotel business that chambermaids were stealing towels from the *guests* . . .**

To you or I, this gag may sound quite funny, but believe me, it's odds-on that every bugger in that room has heard it loads of times.

Try to use your head when you research for a speech. Sometimes you may even improve on the material. Here's an example:

> **A man knocked on Harry Fisher's door in the middle of the night;**
> **'I have good news and bad news', he announced,**
> **'The good news is, you have the right to remain silent . . . '**

I originally saw the joke in this form:

> **The police officer said to the accused;**
> **'I have some good news and some bad news . . .**
> **the good news is, you have the right to remain silent.'**

To me, this wording gave the game away. At the outset, we're told that a police officer is speaking. When I changed it, I felt the effect would be much funnier if 'the right to remain silent' line alone identified the stranger.

The element of surprise is highly important in humour. One-liners usually contain a 'set-up' and a sting. For example:

Set-up: **'I'd love to see her in something long and flowing . . . '**

Sting: **' . . . like a river!'**

The words 'long and flowing' are crucial. They conjure up the image of a beautiful ball gown. The audience has been 'set-up' for the surprise of the 'sting' line. Change these words and you lose the point. Put a line or even one more word between 'flowing' and 'river' and you weaken the impact.

Your audience has to retain the memory of the 'set-up' in order to realise they've been had.

So don't be tempted to embellish a good line.

If it ain't broke, don't fix it!

Equally, if you feel you need to trim a one-liner, make sure that your cut doesn't damage the flow. Sometimes a gag can sound 'one-legged' if the rhythm is disturbed.

Set-up: **'Earlier this evening, at the reception, I met Gerry Marshall; a brilliant lawyer and a real gentleman . . .'**

Sting: **' . . . later on I had drinks with all three of them!'**

The audience readily, but mistakenly, takes on board what they believe is your description of Gerry Marshall.

Suddenly, they hear the words 'all three of them'.

They rewind to 'Gerry Marshall, a brilliant lawyer and a real gentleman', and realise you've conned 'em.

With this one-liner, you'll have to allow for a couple of extra beats before you get your laugh . . . the thought-process often produces a delayed reaction.

Think very carefully before messing about too much with one-liners.

Be aware that certain words, which may appear innocuous or superfluous, could be part of the magic that makes us laugh.

Removing those words may be fatal to the line.

Some words are simply funny words.

For example:

'Hen' – nothing,	'Chicken' – funny.
'Gloves' – nothing,	'Socks' – funny.
'Beige' – nothing,	'Puce' – funny.

Now I hate analysing comedy, it really ruins it. A line is either funny or it isn't, so I'm very sorry, I really must apologise for having to get into all this.

Nevertheless, sometimes an illustration or two may help someone avoid ruining an otherwise effective line and I'm the one landed with the responsibility of pointing you in the right direction.

It's a dirty job, but somebody's got to do it, so to *hell* with it . . . I withdraw my apology!

Chapter Seven

NOTES, SCRIPT OR MEMORY?

Many experts advise against writing your speech out in full.

They feel that this method would make your performance sound false and contrived.

I happen to differ. It ain't necessarily so.

Let's look at the alternatives:

CUE CARDS

To start with, I think these things are distracting and look very silly.

They give the impression that you've hastily jotted down a few words on some old place-cards you found a few minutes ago in the cloak-room.

A five minute speech could contain about fifty cues. At the normal delivery speed, your card shuffling will very rapidly begin to fascinate the audience more than whatever you're saying.

NOTES ON A SHEET OF PAPER

Not too bad a method for some speeches or presentations, but remember – the one-liner format in particular requires precise construction. All sorts of things can go wrong if your notes don't trigger the correct phrasing or if you're not prompted to use the key words.

By the time you've made a note of all the crucial bullet-points, phrased them in the correct order and included the 'magic' necessary for one-liners to work properly, it's hardly worth the bother. You might as well write it out in full.

LEARN IT BY HEART?

Unless you have a photographic memory, a wealth of experience and nerves of steel, forget it! Because chances are, you will!

You're going to be nervous in any case; even the most seasoned professional expects a few butterflies before he or she stands up. Why inflict upon yourself the added terror of forgetting your words?

Believe me, when you stand up to speak, you're going to need as much confidence as you can falsify.

Instead of trying to memorise a fast-moving speech of this kind, you'd do better to utilise some of my sneakier techniques. These little tricks were designed to make the audience almost unaware that you're reading the whole thing.

What's more, they work.

So instead of sitting up night after night, attempting to learn fourteen hundred crucial words, use just a fraction of that time and effort to develop the knack of presenting your speech in a natural and relaxed manner.

Here's what I recommend:

MY COLOURTEXT SYSTEM

Write the speech out in full on reasonably heavy paper, about 7 inches by 9 (17cm x 24). The paper shouldn't be too flimsy as the pages need to be easy to separate as you're reading.

I find block capitals are best; they're much easier to read.

Use felt-tip pens in varying colours, for instance, one joke or small paragraph in blue, the next in green. The following line could be in black, followed by purple, and so on.

Finally, underline certain key words in red. These could be words you need to emphasise, or merely the 'bones' of a line which could be glanced at and used as shorthand.

There's no dishonour in having a script; TV presenters work from fully-worded autocues and cue cards. Politicians read their speeches in full from those invisible reflector things we professionals call – 'invisible reflector things'.

What matters is how you use it. Hang around, I've got tricks.

I'm sure you've seen speechmakers happily reading from typewritten or handwritten sheets of A4. Realising, quite rightly, that they need to look away from the script and make some eye contact with their audience from time to time, they look up and finish a line or two from memory as they glance around the room. Then they look down again . . .

Silence . . . more silence . . . *excruciating* silence.

A desperate and embarrassing search has begun. The poor sap has lost his place!

'Where was I? Up the top? No, I've done that bit. Somewhere about three quarters of the way down, I think . . . er . . .'

Trouble is, all the words on the page look exactly the same. It's just one sheet of writing.

However, with my recommended system of using coloured text, it's much less likely that you'll lose your place.

Don't be concerned; you don't need to memorise the colour you were on before you looked away from your script. For some reason, your subconscious takes care of all that. It usually leads you back to the correct place.

Practise it. Even if it doesn't work for you one hundred per cent, at least you'll be able to scan the page at a faster rate.

Remember, you only have to look at the beginning of each topic to know whether it's the right one or not, and you ought only to have about eight to ten one-liners per page.

As I said at the beginning of the chapter on editing, the

one-liner construction makes it much easier to cut whole sections of your speech in 'real-time' if necessary.

The colourtext system makes it easier still.

Chapter Eight

A VERY SNEAKY PLOY

Here's a little trick to make people unaware that, in fact, you're reading your speech word for word.

Start off with a couple of announcements – it's perfectly natural for you to be reading these – then you can go straight into your speech, still reading, and they won't even notice.

Ladies and Gentlemen, before I start, I've been asked to make the following announcements:

We've arranged a couple of extra items for you this evening. A little later on, Stephen Lowe of Her Majesty's Customs and Excise is going to be coming on to show us all how to fill in one of the new VAT forms . . .

After that, Mr Dominic Riley – a self-employed builder – will be coming on to show us all how to fill in Stephen Lowe.

I'm happy to announce that our treasurer, Frank Stanton, is celebrating a *double* birthday today. Frank is fifty . . . and his hair is twenty-nine!

Incidentally the Heritage Secretary has just declared Frank Stanton's toupee a National Wildlife Sanctuary.

One word of warning though . . . don't stand too near Frank immediately after he's been dancing . . .
When he over-heats, you can get *high* from the glue in his wig!

Ladies and gentlemen, this evening is a very special night for all of us . . .

. . . and you're into the speech.

People are now quite used to seeing you glancing down at the paper, and, as long as you bring your head up and look around the room regularly as you speak, they won't be conscious of you reading from a script.

By the way, during your speech, always make sure your next page is ready for you well before you come to the end of your current page.

Chapter Nine

THIS TIME, EVEN DHL CAN'T HELP YOU WITH YOUR DELIVERY

Making a speech for the first time is very much like making love for the first time. Because you may not have total confidence in what you're doing, the temptation is to rush it.

She's going to change her mind . . . I'm going to lose it . . . we're going to be interrupted . . .

Oh.

You don't really know for sure whether your speech is going to be well received or not.

Is the material funny enough? Is that one-liner in poor taste?

Am I trying too hard?

Your audience will be slower to react at the beginning of your piece than at the end. Although you may know each one of them really well as individuals, together they have become an audience and you have become a speaker. As such you're new to each other.

You need to re-assess your relationship.

You need to learn about them as an audience, and they – in turn – need to get the hang of you as a speaker. That's why they're liable to be slower at the beginning of your speech than they will be at the end.

Rushing into the next line too early is a sign that you are losing your nerve. Control it.

Don't be shy about laughing at your own jokes occasionally – it further bonds you with your audience. In a way, you're saying, 'What a daft gag, let's enjoy it together'.

Don't ever announce an upcoming joke or one-liner . . . it's a cop out. You are attempting to discard responsibility should it fail.

As you deliver a line, wait just a little before you jump in with the next. As I illustrated earlier, sometimes a gag will produce a delayed reaction and by the time the laughter builds up to its peak, you're halfway through the next line if you're not careful. So let the laughter run its course, and when it's just beginning to taper off, come in strong with the next gag.

You have to be sensible about this, of course. Don't stand up there in total silence. If a joke dies, bury it with the next.

If you're in a large room – a conference centre, for instance – your style should be slightly more elaborate, the expressions you use should be bigger, your language should be a tad less casual.

You'll also find that, for some strange reason, the laughter will radiate away from you in waves. People in the first few rows will seem to react to your gags well before those at the back.

I can't explain this phenomenon. I can only assure you that the effect has nothing to do with the speed of sound. So be even more careful with your pace and learn to allow for this bizarre delay.

Be prepared for an occasional burst of applause.

It's a great compliment.

The audience are telling you they think you're clever and they're grateful you took the trouble to offer them such a good line. Spontaneous applause usually happens when a joke is 'right on the button', or if you've come up with a timely topical gag.

If all goes well, by the time you're about halfway through the speech, you'll find that you are actually conducting the audience as you would an orchestra.

Don't feel guilty; they love being controlled.

In showbusiness, there's a technical name for people who really know how to manipulate their audiences:

Stars.

Chapter Ten

HELLO MIKE!

You'll be reading from a full script, so you'll need both hands available throughout your speech.

One hand will be holding the paper, the other will need to be free for page-turning, gestures, slide operation, water-sipping, toasting or – should you insult the wrong guy – self-defence.

It's almost essential, therefore, to ensure you have a free-standing microphone. I prefer a table stand, but any mike stand will do.

You'll have to arrange for this in advance.

Don't trust to luck and don't believe people who tell you to leave it all to them. It's your responsibility.

You're the one who'll look awkward if things are not right.

Don't test the mike by blowing on it or saying, 'One two, one two!' If you do, I'll come over there and knock your bloody block off myself! Right?

Just tap the mike gently to make sure it's working. If it's not, get someone to switch it on.

Speak from the table or from within the crowd if you can. Avoid speaking from the stage, unless you're there as a platform guest. The stage becomes a barrier between you and the audience and interferes with that special intimate relationship.

Instead of speaking as part of the crowd, the platform or dance floor makes it a case of 'us and them' and you won't get the results your material deserves.

When you speak, speak loudly, speak clearly and speak with confidence. After all, you can afford to speak with confidence when your material is strong, and it will be ... stick around.

Chapter Eleven

BOOZE ... J'ACCUSE!

When you speak at a social occasion, it normally matters very little whether the crowd remembers your words the next day, or forgets the whole thing. The aftermath of a business speech, however, can be crucial. Crucial to your product, to your company, or to your career.

You are aiming for a lasting impression and a residual effect.

Your speech alone is not the whole story.

The memory of the event itself – and your part in it – may linger on, sometimes for years.

Needless to say, your priority is to do all you can do in making sure that image is a positive one.

Many business speakers have flushed away promising careers by going over the top with inappropriate language, bad taste and other undignified behaviour.

It happens a lot.

Sooner or later, you're going to have to make a frank self-assessment of how you behave when under the influence of alcohol, but that's not my problem. For the time being, I want to concentrate solely on the effect of alcohol upon the speech you'll be making.

(Oh shut up! – I'm not going to tell you not to drink!)

While you're waiting to speak, level with yourself . . .

- are you slurring words?

- are you liable to sway?

- or see double? . . . or burp? . . . or worse?

If the answer to any of these questions is 'yeshh', don't be too alarmed. At least you've proved that the alcohol is working properly.

However, as a speechmaker, you have a problem.

You must switch immediately to water.

I know, I know, it's horrible stuff, and yes, I do realise what fishes do in it, but you've swallowed too much poison and water is the antidote.

Trust me, my brother-in-law's a dentist!

(Mind you, that's all water under the bridge.)

Drink as much water as you can as fast as you can, whether you feel like it or not.

Inevitably you'll suddenly find yourself doing a lot of travelling, but that's just nature's way of helping the water to circulate around your system. You should be straightened out within ten to fifteen minutes, but keep that water handy. You'll need it during your speech, and here's why:

Nerves have a really interesting effect upon an inexperienced speaker.

Your mouth suddenly dries up. It feels like someone has stuffed a ball of blotting paper into it.

As you try to speak, your tongue sticks to the roof of your mouth and you suddenly wish you had Teflon gums!

It's a most peculiar phenomenon and one which requires a good supply of water most of the way through your speech.

But let's turn this into an advantage . . .

Use the glass of water as a prop. It can have the same effect as the late George Burns' cigar – a punctuation device assisting in the control of your audience.

After you hit 'em with a one-liner, take a drink while they're laughing – don't worry, most of the material in this book is strong enough to give you enough time to have a gargle! After a while, you'll find the crowd will begin to co-operate with you by stretching out their laughs until you've finished drinking.

People really are dumb, aren't they?

NB: Don't forget, once your speech is over, go straight back to alcohol. After all, you don't want to make a habit of this water thing, do you? Just think, if water can rot the soles of your shoes, imagine what it can do to your stomach!

Chapter Twelve

READY TO ROLL

Before you start rehearsing your speech, check it over one more time. Ask yourself a few questions:

- Does my speech have a good opening?

- Does it have the right amount of humour for the occasion?

- Does it have the right *style* of humour for the occasion?

- Does it have the right style of humour for the *audience*?

- Does the speech get my message across in a memorable way?

- Is it the right length?

- Where did I put it?

Once you've found it again, rehearse at the correct pace. Imagine the laughter and allow time for it.

Put in your own light and shade. You may need to deliver some passages quite gently . . . at other times, you'll be shouting.

Make sure it all rings true. Don't over-dramatise – you're not a luvvie, you're a dude!

Are you totally comfortable with the material?

Are you stumbling over certain words or phrases? If so, change them, but make sure you don't kill the line.

If in doubt, cut it out.

Rehearse three or four times in a row, then leave it alone.

Rehearse again shortly before you leave for the venue.

Take a couple of coloured pens with you for any last-minute alterations or cuts.

Go to an appropriate room and freshen up before it's time for you to speak.

Be confident. Your material is SENSATIONAL!

Chapter Thirteen

GET THE MAX

Okay, let's not jerk around any longer with all that important stuff. It's time we got silly and made a start with the first of our one-liners.

Many of the lines in this book are interchangeable. Keep an eye open for easily adaptable jokes. For instance, you will find the following quip under 'Accountants':

> **But I really don't want to make too many accountant jokes tonight . . . I think the facts speak for themselves . . .**

However, the line works equally well with any other profession or position worth making fun of . . . hospital administrators, town planners, tax inspectors.

Under 'Advertising', you'll find the line:

> **Advertising is the science of arresting the human intelligence long enough to get money from it!**

You could just as easily say:

Pop music is the art of arresting the human emotion long enough to get money from it!

(And, as an old pop songwriter, I should know.)

I call these adaptable gags 'Flexi Lines' and I've marked quite a few of them as such.

However, interchangeable lines come up so often that, if you want to gain maximum advantage from these pages, I'm afraid you're going to have to read the whole damn book after all.

Sorry.

Dorothy Parker, the great American humorist, wrote:

'There are those who, in their pride and their innocence, dedicate their careers to writing humorous pieces.

Poor dears, the world is stacked against them from the start, for everybody in it has the right to look at their work and say, 'I don't think that's funny'.'

Well, for God's sake, there are nearly a thousand one-liners in this book. You must be able to find *something* you like!

Chapter Fourteen

WELCOME TO ONE-LINER LAND

Let's start with an anti-climax.

ACCOUNTANTS, FINANCE DIRECTORS
and other electrifying personalities

An accountant is usually a mild, inoffensive man . . . but then, of course, so was Crippen!

In any case, I don't think it's valid to bunch all accountants into stereotypes . . . these people are monotypes!

Ladies and gentlemen . . . just once in a lifetime, someone in my position has the opportunity to introduce a man blessed with dynamic charisma, devastating wit, great talent and an unstoppable personality . . . but until the day that one comes along, we have Howard Nicholls.

Like most accountants, he's a very meticulous man . . . he even eats his alphabet soup in alphabetical order!

What an accountant! He's a ledger in his own lifetime.

Old accountants never die . . . they just lose their balance.

There are three types of accountant . . . those who can count and those who can't.

Watching two accountants walking along together is quite a sight . . . the bland leading the bland.

As a Finance Director, he's always being asked for his advice . . . obviously, people are too bloody lazy to come up with their own ideas for losing money.

Noah is the Patron Saint of accounting . . . he employed a double-entry system in order to float a limited company while the rest of the world was in liquidation!

But I really don't want to make too many accountant jokes tonight . . . I think the facts speak for themselves . . .

(Flexi line)

In any case, we're lucky to have Howard Nicholls as our accountant. The tax people have just paid a him a great compliment . . . they've named a loophole after him!

I don't know if you noticed, but earlier, when they toasted 'Absent Friends', Howard Nicholls stood up and took a bow!

This man has that certain . . . nothing!

His father looks upon him as the son he never had!

He may *seem* insignificant, but there really is a lot less to him than meets the eye!

It's pathetic really. Once, when Howard was drowning, his whole life flashed before his eyes . . . and he wasn't in it!

When they made Howard, they kept the mould and threw *him* away!

At first, when this guy walked into the office, I thought it was Howard Nicholls . . . but then I realised it was just a case of mistaken nonentity!

In the Auditor's Hall of Fame, Howard Nicholls is honoured by a blank plaque.

His motto is: 'Be it ever so humble, there's no place like a tax shelter'.

I have good news and bad news.
First the bad news . . . in a moment or two, our Treasurer, Tony Reynolds will be reading us the financial report.

The good news is . . . he's not 'phoning it in from Brazil!

ADVERTISING

The codfish lays ten thousand eggs, the homely hen lays one.
The codfish never cackles to tell you what she's done.
And so we scorn the codfish while the humble hen we prize,
Which only goes to show you that it pays to advertise.

You may have noticed that CNN – the news station that makes you sit through hours of pompous internationalist crap for the sake of a few magic moments of excellence, runs a regular commercial which devotes itself to advertising . . . advertising.

Its tag line is: 'Advertising – the right to choose'.

What it really means is – the 'right to choose' from those few companies who can afford to spend millions on their campaigns.

Despite all those organizations monitoring advertising standards, can we really rely on some of the claims they make? After all, it's a little worrying when you buy a tube of superglue and as soon as you get home, the label falls off.

. . . But if you think *I'm* cynical, read what George Orwell had to say on the subject:

'Advertising is the rattling of a stick inside a swill bucket.'

I somehow get the feeling that old George was not very impressed with the world of advertising. Never mind, the world of advertising needn't be too impressed with Orwell . . . have you read 1984?
Nostradamus he ain't!

On to the one-liners.

We start with a slogan I came up with for a funeral parlour in California:

'Have a nice death'

(. . . they didn't use it, so I offered it to Murder Inc. – I'm still waiting to hear).

Advertising is the art of making you think you've longed all your life for something you've never heard of before.

If you don't believe that advertising works, think about the millions of people who are convinced that yoghurt tastes good.

(Bridging line)

Sign in a Cambridge bookshop: 'Read a good novel before Hollywood screws it up'.

(Bridging line)

Doing business without advertising is like winking at a girl in the dark . . . you know what you're doing, but she doesn't.

Samson would have made a wonderful show business publicist . . . he took two columns and brought the house down.

Advertising is the science of arresting the human intelligence just long enough to get money from it!

(Flexi line)

The nice thing about the advertising business is that it really keeps you fit . . . every lunch hour you're out looking for another job!

(Bridging Line) (Flexi line)

The truly efficient publicist should be able to hype ninety words a minute.

Slogan: 'Ears pierced. We pick up and deliver.'

When the client moans and sighs,
Make his logo twice the size.
If he still should prove refractory,
Show a picture of his factory.
Only in the gravest cases
Should you show the clients' faces.

. . . try telling *that* to Victor Kiam.

One account executive to another . . .
'Hello Robin. What's new and improved?'

The only outfit I know capable of making money without advertising is the Royal Mint.

Sign in a curio shop: 'Junk bought – Antiques sold.'

Advertising agency MD: 'Young man, your CV is filled with half-truths, inaccuracies and misleading information. When can you start?'

When it comes to health claims, a company like Burger King can't afford any hint that there may be a lie involved in their publicity . . .
So what Clever Dick thought up the name – 'Whopper'?

(See also 'The Media')

ADVICE

If you hit mid-life crisis and suddenly feel the need to 'find yourself', why not start with the Yellow Pages?
. . . it could save you years.

Advice to the company man – always aim high . . . that way you won't splash your shoes.

If you can tell the difference between good advice and bad advice, you don't need advice.

Remember, never argue with a fool . . . he may be doing the same thing.

The worst bit of advice he ever got was 'Be yourself'.

Don't ever ask directions from a postman . . . I tried it once. He said, 'Go straight down until you get to WC1 AJR, turn left at WC4 8RS, left again at EC5 1JP and make a right into EC2 3BT'.

I could give you all sorts of advice but I won't . . . you can't afford my advice!

If 'a' equals success, then the formula is 'a' equals 'x' plus 'y' plus 'z'.
'x' is work, 'y' is play, 'z' is keep your mouth shut.

(Albert Einstein)

(Between you and me, I couldn't make any sense out of his $E=MC^2$ either.)

Never give advice . . . Sell it!

Young man . . . make good, or make room.

I don't know why they make such a performance about oil slicks. Here's a simple formula for getting rid of them . . .
Pour on several thousand gallons of vinegar and then drop giant croutons to soak up the spill.

Always look out for number one and be careful not to step in number two!

Isn't it funny how top businessmen ignore their assistant's advice and pay consultants £300 an hour to tell them the same thing?

A good scare is worth more to a man than good advice.
(Ed Howe)

The only place where success comes before work . . .
is in the dictionary!

I'd like to end my speech with a piece of advice . . .
never end a speech with a piece of advice!

(See also 'Experts and Consultants')

AMBITION

My great ambition is to live to be as old as some the material
in this book.

Confucius he say . . .
'To be top dog, you must first be son-of-a-bitch'.

Ambition means working yourself to death so you can
live better.

How many young men who leave home to set the world
on fire, have to come back for more matches?

When he was a kid, his burning desire was to become
a pirate. Now, he's a lawyer. He's lucky . . . very few
people realise their ambition.
(Bridging line) (Flexi line)

Ambition: A poor excuse for not having sense enough
to be lazy.

Once upon a time it was ambition that kept people on the move . . . now it's the threat of a wheel clamp.

(Bridging line)

AWARDS, PRIZES AND TROPHIES
GIVING 'EM . . .

You may remember that last year, Joe Draper walked away with all the awards . . . luckily, security caught him at the door and made him put them back!

First prize in our 'Budget-Beaters' contest *next* year, is an all-expenses paid trip to the Falkland Islands with the sheep of your choice!

I have good news and bad news for Joe Draper . . . the good news is that he's just won a major national competition.
The bad news . . . a little worrying . . . it was a Salman Rushdie look-alike contest!

Mark Twain said: 'It is better to deserve prizes and not have them, than to have them and not deserve them'.
With this in mind, the following people will be proud, I'm sure, not to be receiving prizes this evening . . .

Read a list of names . . .

Congratulations, all of you.

And now a man whose 1985 tax return was nominated for the 'Inland Revenue Comedy Award'! . . .

You know Jack, as I look at this trophy, I honestly can't imagine it going to anyone else . . .
especially as your name's engraved on the bloody thing!

I'm delighted to announce that Joe Draper has been awarded 'Freedom of the City . . .
In case any of you would like to be there, the presentation will be taking place next week in the city itself . . . Beirut!

GETTING 'EM...

I'd like to thank the members of the Academy for this award . . . oh no, sorry, that was the wrong speech!

Thank you all for this wonderful award . . .
I can certainly promise you that I will cherish it until the end of time . . . or 'Newsweek', whichever subscription expires first!

I'd put this on my mantlepiece with my other awards . . . if I *had* any other awards . . .
if I had a *mantlepiece*!

Thank you very much . . . this makes up for all those times that bastard Pulitzer overlooked me!

Thank you for this award. At this time of my life, I just can't tell you how much it means to me . . . but I should have a better idea on Monday, once I've spoken to the guy in the pawn shop!

This isn't false modesty, but I do get the feeling that standards are definitely slipping . . . I hear that next year's favourite to win the Booker Prize is the south-facing wall of a Gentleman's Toilet in the Bus Station at Brighton.

They say that 'modesty' is the art of drawing attention to whatever it is you're being humble about . . .
Well, tonight I feel very modest . . . as modest as a peacock!
Thank you all . . . have a great evening.

(See also 'Retirement' and 'The Tribute')

BAD NEWS

The treatment of bad news in your speech should, of course, be handled with a great deal of care.

During a crisis, your audience will be wondering:

* What exactly has happened?
* How will it affect me?
* What's being done about it?

The use of humour is as tricky as Dicky when it comes to unpleasant tidings. It could so easily backfire if your audience feels you are being too flippant about a serious state of affairs.

My suggestion is to use humour only in order to keep the situation in perspective or as a link to other topics.

It's easy to say business is improving . . .
Saying it with a straight *face* is the problem.

According to the Annual Report, one of the few projects that was completed this year was . . . the . . . Annual . . . Report.

I'm not going to go into that; it's so sad . . . I might cry and dilute my brandy!

(Bridging line)

I don't really want to comment on the latest figures, but I think I should take this opportunity of announcing our proposed new logo . . .
it's a picture of a canoe without a paddle!

Here's more bad news . . . that was my best joke!

I'd like to say that next year looks like being our best ever . . . *Boy*, would I like to say that!

I don't want this conference centre to be thought of as a house of ill report, but . . .

You know you're in a recession when the Salvation Army Soup Kitchens start serving Businessman's Lunches.

This year, in time for our AGM, we've decided to have our Annual Report written by a professional . . . Stephen King!

I have good news and bad news. First, the good news . . . Ian Parkin is going to sing for us all . . . and that'll give you some idea of how bad the *bad* news is!

These figures prove that not all the suffering is in the Third World.

BAD PAYERS

. . . whose cheques may not actually *bounce*, but they certainly twitch a little.

They honour their debts . . . every month, they award a trophy to the creditor who's been waiting around the longest.

He said we'd have to wait for payment because, at the moment, all his money is tied up in debt.

He always travels First Class . . . that way he avoids his creditors.

He once went bankrupt, took a taxi to his court case and had the cheek to bring the driver in as a creditor!

He complained that we ask too much for the rent. He's right . . . last month we had to ask five times!

No man's credit is as good as his money . . .

They promised they'd pay us in three days . . . They did! . . . January 5th, July 14th and December 3rd!

Most of their creditors have one thing in common . . . nothing.

(See also 'Spivs')

BALD HEADS AND HAIRY WIGS

Announcement: Will the owner of Toupee, Serial number 727318, kindly collect it from the foyer . . . it's beginning to confuse the cat!

He suffers from the same problems as my house . . . a thinning roof, a sagging foundation and clogged pipes.

Anytime now, he'll be losing his hair . . . unless he keeps up the payments on it!

This is a man who proves that a hair in the head is worth two in the brush.

He used to have lovely wavy hair, but then one day, it waved bye bye! . . . (it was a sad parting).

I always said he'd come out on top.

(Bridging line)

At school he was voted: 'The boy most likely to recede'.

One of the main problems facing manufacturers these days is not production . . . it's distribution. This comes home to Frank Stanton every time he shaves.

Why does he buy such cheap toupees? . . . these days he's losing hair that isn't even *his*!

(*More toupee lines in Chapter Eight*)

BASTARDS

Stan Pearce happened to be a premature baby . . . he was born three months before his parents got married!

. . . Which qualifies him for the title role in this section.

Ladies and gentlemen, I've always believed that if you can't say something good about someone, you're probably talking about Stan Pearce.

This guy doesn't waste words . . . everything he has to say can be summed up in one finger.

Stan Pearce has been called stubborn, inconsiderate, arrogant, untrustworthy and selfish . . . and let's face it, a mother should know!

He's an only child . . . his parents decided to stop while they still outnumbered him!

He's just been named by the British Medical Association as an honorary disease!

He's listed in the Guinness Book of Yechhhh!

He's still his own worse enemy, but the competition's getting stiffer all the time.

His conscience is clean . . . it *should* be clean . . . he's never used it!

If you lend him money, you'll never see him again . . . and it's worth it!

He never loses his temper . . . it's always right there.

Our business relationship has never been the same since I told him his bark was worse than his bite and he bit me.

He's a family man . . . but then, of course, so was Charles Manson.

He likes to put women on a pedestal . . . then he pushes them in and flushes them away!

He's a contrary sonofabitch. After dinner, when everybody else orders port . . . he orders starboard!

(Bridging line)

But Stan's got loads of pals . . . Christ – he's got friends he hasn't even *used* yet!

I don't like him, and I always will.

BEREAVEMENT AND ILLNESS

There's always a danger, when handling certain sensitive issues such as serious illness or recent bereavement, that your audience will become sombre and that your speech will end on a sad and awkward note.

BEREAVEMENT

The sudden loss of a well-loved associate has to be acknowledged by at least one of the speakers.

If this situation is not handled with care, the speechmaker risks 'losing' his or her audience during what would otherwise have been a sparkling, laugh-a-minute extravaganza.

It's almost enough to make you wish they hadn't passed away, isn't it?

I always place these subjects about three quarters of the way through the speech, giving the speechmaker plenty of time to ease out of the poignant atmosphere and back, gently, into the laughter.

Of course, the language you use is crucial. Avoid words like 'dead', 'killed', 'injured', 'terminal', 'senseless', etc., and substitute gentler and more positive language.

Try to portray the departed with a semblance of continuity. Here's an example:

> **You know, it's remarkable how absence can have an impact of its own.**
> **When an old cherished friend is missing from a gathering of colleagues, it really is very noticeable.**

Earlier this year — sadly — we lost our Marketing Director, Gerry Baldwin and, although we miss him a lot, in a special sort of way he's still sitting here with us tonight, joining in with the toasts and laughing at the jokes.

Such is the effect Gerry continues to have upon those of us who enjoyed working with him.

Of course, Gerry Baldwin was also a husband and a father, and we're all delighted to have Jayne Baldwin with us tonight, looking so good and in such great form.

(Expect applause)

I must say, it's *particularly* gratifying that Jayne decided to come along and share the evening with us, despite the fact that she knew full well I'd be making a speech.

Brave woman!

The whole idea is that the lines get lighter gradually so that you don't have an unseemly leap from sadness to hilarity.

However tragic the circumstances of Gerry's death, you'll notice that, while not in any way trivialising his passing, the words are totally natural and he is treated in a straightforward manner, almost as if he were on holiday.

This way, we've shown respect and affection for our absent colleague, we've kept the audience from drifting into depression and we're ready to go straight into another series of one-liners before closing the speech.

ILLNESS

Treat all illnesses as transient.

This doesn't mean you should belittle other people's health problems, but bear in mind that each sufferer handles his or her condition differently.

Be safe. Acknowledge it, but don't dwell on it.

This sort of thing should be fine:

> **We're all very happy to see Brenda Maley back with us this afternoon, looking fit as a fiddle after her recent operation.**

(Expect applause)

> **Brenda, we're thrilled you were able to make it today and it's good to see that you're obviously well on the road to recovery.**

Here's a form of wording which may be suitable for those who are absent through illness:

> **I'm sure you'll all be pleased to hear that both Alf Thompson and Brian Castle have come through their tough battles and are now well and truly on the mend – they really don't make streetfighters like those two any more do they?**

Or, if the news isn't so bright:

If there's one person who can weather this particularly nasty storm, I know it's Deborah . . . our thoughts tonight are with her and her family and we all look forward to seeing her back in action and, as usual, taking no prisoners.

Needless to say, I have no one-liners for you in this section.

BOOZE 'N' BOOZERS

It's estimated there are one million alcoholics in this country . . .
These are staggering figures!

For those who are interested, there's a new support group: 'Teetotalers Anonymous'. If you feel like going on the wagon, you call a Freephone number and two drunks come over and try to talk you out of it.

Sign on the wall in a Chelsea bar: 'If you're drinking to forget, please pay in advance'.

If you drink before you drive, you're putting the quart before the hearse.

This year's new trendy drink is called 'Autumn Leaf' – you take one sip, change colour and fall to the ground!

When I was a kid, my grandfather was known as the town drunk . . . and we lived in Manchester!

I remember every Saturday morning he used to go down to the Blood Bank to get his eyes drained.

Who can forget that crazy night he took his trousers down to moon . . . and the cow jumped over *him*!?

A lot of people drink claret with their meal, but . . . breakfast!?

He has a very strained relationship with his body. In fact, he's on the verge of splitting up . . . claims his liver doesn't understand him.

One of the best things you can do is to drink a lot when you get old. That way, every time you go to kick the bucket, you miss!

(Bridging line)

At least he's a happy drinker . . . always laughing and shaking hands . . . even when he's alone!

He drinks just to pass the time . . . last night, he passed 1999!

Most of the time, he doesn't drink anything stronger than pop . . . mind you, Pop'll drink *anything*!

When I tried to bring my own wine into the place, they charged me corkage! . . . cost me three corks!

I'm perfectly all right. *You're* the one who's spinning around!

I'll never forget the night we all went out and got sober.

He drinks to forget . . . he drinks to forget his *future*!

This guy is a connoisseur of wine. He can tell from one sip, not only the year it was made, not only the vineyard . . . but he can tell you the bust measurement of the bird who jumped on the bloody grapes!

(Bridging line)

He's not really a big drinker . . . he donated his body to science and he's merely preserving it in alcohol until they use it!

He's trying to be a bit more environmentally friendly with his drinking these days . . . he's already switched from regular Bacardi to Diesel.

(Bridging line)

BORES

Generally speaking, these people are – generally – speaking.

Due to popular demand, Sidney Stafford will *not* be making a speech tonight.

Our newest company car comes with an airbag . . . but enough about Sidney.

(Bridging line)

The Department of Health has just announced that Sidney Stafford has now been cleared for use as an approved sedative.

When he's in full flow, all I do is say 'Wow!' every now and then . . . it's not very clever, but it fits a yawn perfectly.

He'd make a great Governor of the Bank of England . . . whenever he speaks, everyone's interest rate drops.

When you're having a conversation with this man, believe me, there's never a dull moment . . . it lasts all the way through.

How do you manage to spend an evening with Sidney Stafford? One idea is to paint open eyes on your glasses!

I may not agree with what he says, but I'll defend to the *death*, the right of somebody to shut him up!

OK, so his mind wanders a bit, but be fair . . . wouldn't you if *you* were in that body?

(Bridging line)

THE BOSS

. . . that infuriating man at the office who's early when you're late, and late when you're early.

The boss is your client. He's purchasing your services. Every time you get paid, it means your employer has re-ordered.

So, in the same way you should always remember your customer is boss, never forget that the boss is your customer. Treat him as such.

When referring to corporate superiors, don't be misled by the easy-going personal manner they may seem to have in private. There is a big difference between one-to-one banter and public ribbing. Personally, they may not be offended, but they could start to worry about the reactions of others who may be embarrassed on their behalf. If you appear to take too many verbal liberties, onlookers may well start to wonder about your company's power structure.

However close to someone you may be, don't risk saying anything inappropriate in front of an audience.

As James Thurber once said:

'A man should not insult his wife publicly, at parties. He should insult her in the privacy of the home.'

Of course a boss is not as lethal as a wife but you know what I'm getting at. If you don't, you've never been married.

Should you wish to play totally safe with lines about your corporate superiors, stay with positive humour. Needless to say, the same advice also applies to remarks about your clients.

Joke about your boss's power, his wealth, his influence, his toughness. Try 'The Tribute' section for examples of these 'winner' lines.

If you are male and your superior is female, don't patronise her.

Don't fall over yourself trying to be politically correct – just treat her with the respect her position entitles her to. It's important that you appear totally at ease with the situation. Gender, as such, should not be an issue. Nevertheless, your material needs to be scrupulously tasteful.

Check out my 'Women In Business' and 'Political Correctitude' sections.

Later in this book, in the section on 'Roasts and Insults', I introduce my own devilishly clever device known as 'Safe Slander'. This could be a useful technique for anyone wishing to navigate that treacherous channel between sycophancy and insubordination. You may wish to adopt these principles in order to distance yourself from the directness of the material, but don't kid yourself that you'll be fooling anyone. It's just that, with a protective extra psychological tier, you have a better chance of getting away with it.

And if you understood that last line, you obviously don't get out enough.

Here are some 'governor lines' – some positive, some negative. There are also some lines to use if the boss is *you*.

I shall call the boss 'David Carter'.

David and I make a great team ... I do everything ... and he does the rest!

We have only two rules here;
One – Dave Carter is always right, and . . .
Two – When Dave Carter is wrong, refer to Rule One.

David Carter has just been appointed Chairman of the Board, an honour very few people receive while they're still alive.

Question: What's the difference between David Carter and the Pope?
Answer: You only have to kiss the Pope's ring.

Ancient legend has it, that when a baby is born, it's guardian angel kisses it.
If it's kissed on the head, it'll become a philosopher or an academic . . . if it's kissed on the lips, it'll become a great orator or communicator . . . if it's kissed on the hands, it'll become a great musician or a sculptor . . . Now I don't know where David Carter was kissed, but he's certainly a great chairman!

I must say he's a brilliant man to have at the helm. I must say that; he *told* me I must.

Despite all the jokes, David is really very sentimental. In fact, I happen to know that he has the heart of a small boy . . . keeps it in a jar in his garage!

One day last summer, he had a very nasty accident . . . he was out, taking his usual walk, and he got hit by a motorboat!

Question: What's the difference between God and David Carter?
Answer: God doesn't think he's David Carter.

I'd like to tell you about all his accomplishments as chairman . . . have you got a second?

Here's an interesting question: Is it necessarily true that every time a chief executive stubs his toe in Bosnia, it Herzogovina?

Show me a man who's a good loser . . . and I'll show you a man who plays golf with his boss!

(Bridging line)

There's something a bit impersonal about an organization this size. Only this morning I told my secretary, 'If the boss calls, try to make sure you get his name'.

Or . . .

. . . IF THE BOSS IS YOU

Phil Gorman and I have a very healthy working relationship . . .
With us, everything's done on a fifty-fifty basis . . .
I tell him what to do . . . and he tells me where to go!

I probably wouldn't work for me . . . I wouldn't like my attitude.

I simply can't bear to see my secretary doing all that tedious work . . . so I usually go and have a drink.

As you will have gathered, I think the world of my team . . .
Nevertheless, many people seem to look upon me in awe and find me somewhat intimidating . . .
they all say, 'awwww . . . he's somewhat intimidating'.

You may be unaware of what 'vice chairman' actually means . . .
It's a title they give you instead of a pay rise.

I tell my employees, 'The door to my office is always open . . . so keep your bloody voice down as you go past!'

I'm a self-made man . . . and it nearly made me go blind!

Believe me, I came up the hard way . . . British Rail!
(Bridging line)

To illustrate my point, gentlemen, I'm going to tell you a little story and I want you to laugh as if your job depended on it . . . because it does.

BUDGETS

Balance your budget . . . rotate your creditors!

Living on a budget is the same as living beyond your means, except that you keep a record of it!

A budget is a work of fiction with an unhappy ending.

Budgeting is a system of going into debt in an orderly fashion.

If that's your idea of a budget, you can budge it where the sun don't shine!

BUSY, BUSY, BUSY!

This section is devoted to the guy who's currently leading the field in the Single-Handed Round-The-World Rat Race!

. . . let's call him Max Muir.

Nobody travels as widely as this man . . .
Prague, Singapore, Moscow . . .
In fact, last Friday, three planes landed at Heathrow and Max Muir got off all three of 'em!

This guy has so much adrenalin, that when he dies, at his wake, he'll be able to mingle with the guests!

He just flew in from Brussels . . .
Yeah, that's how hard they kicked him out!

He's been travelling a hell of a lot this year . . .
Athens, Montevideo, Papua New Guinea . . . these are the only three places he *hasn't* been to!

He's so wild, cocaine sniffs *him*!

CARS AND DRIVERS

Andy Wilson really has the Midas touch . . . everything he touches turns into an exhaust system!

He doesn't drink at all, but the police still give him a lot of hassle . . . they just can't believe that *anyone* could drive like that when they're sober.

When the police stop him, not only do they make him blow up a balloon, he then has to twist it into the shape of a giraffe!

He was once nicked for speeding . . .
The policeman was making note of the fact that Andy was doing fifty-five in a built-up area . . .
Andy said, 'Do you think you could make that eighty? I'm trying to sell the car'.

(Bridging line)

I wish people would stop going on about the way he handles a car . . .
For God's sake, if you don't like the way he drives, get off the bloody pavement!'

CHARITY

Many companies nowadays are associating themselves with favourite charitable causes.

Charities may benefit as a result of company-sponsored fund-raising dinners, sporting events, or simply from the proceeds of one-off donations.

Sometimes there is an obvious connection between the firm's activities and the charity itself. For example, a musical instrument manufacturer may wish to support a musician's benevolent association, or a tobacco company may give financial aid to certain areas of medical research.

In other cases, a PR motive may lie behind this kind of philanthropic gesture, or – quite simply – a few good people decide to get together and raise money for a pet cause.

One large company I know is so anxious to get into charity, they've already collected almost two million pounds . . . now they've got to go out and find a disease.

Whatever the background, you may well need the occasional tribute line or humorous quip.

I'll start with some selected passages you may be able to incorporate into your own presentation. As with all excerpts in this book, the sample segments are offered here mainly in order to give you an idea of the appropriate tone and language style for this kind of speech and, possibly, a little inspiration to kick you off.

SAMPLE SPEECH SEGMENTS

Guest speaker at Charity Dinner

It's easy to see that a tremendous amount of work has gone towards making tonight's function a success. I'm sure that you, my fellow guests, will want to be generous in your support this evening; it's the best possible way we can show our gratitude to all those who put so much effort and love into this project.

Opening a Charity Bazaar

I'm sure that the members of Armadale House, their teachers and everyone involved in organising today's bazaar, must feel very gratified to see so many eager faces with one common purpose: to spend in a reckless frenzy!

I can see you're all desperate to do just that, so the very least I can do right now . . . and I do it with great pleasure . . . is to declare this year's Armadale Charity Bazaar open!

Excerpt from President's speech

When you ask the question, 'What does Dorothy Baker do for the club? . . . the answer comes back, 'only everything!'

Officially, she's our General Secretary, but believe me, without her, The Golden Journey Club just wouldn't exist!

She also happens to be the lady who instructed me not to speak for more than three minutes, so you see, she's looking after *your* interests too.

I'm very proud to be associated with The Golden Journey Club and I'll tell you why. You see, I'm just old enough to remember the days when 'charity' was a virtue and not an industry.

Too often, nowadays, charity begins at home . . . and then ends up in some foreign country.

This appeal is quite different . . . the money we raise stays right here and helps to support various deserving causes of our own. The Golden Journey Club is flexible enough to respond year by year, through the National Alderman's Appeal, to varying needs throughout the community.
We may be asked to comfort, we may be asked to feed, to clothe, to warm, to protect, or – this year – to restore.

For ninety-nine years, thanks to the generosity of people like you, we've been able to respond when called upon.
Next year, of course, is our centennial year and we're expecting great things. It's going to be a very special twelve months and we'll have a pretty full programme, so please get your orders in really early for the brochure.

For our one hundredth year, I'm not going to waste my time asking you to 'give till it hurts' . . . that's for wimps!
I'm going to be asking you to give until you find yourself in Intensive Care!

Ladies and gentlemen, whether you advertise in our brochure, buy tombola tickets, make donations or simply come along and support our functions – we're very grateful for your help. Believe me, you really are making a difference.

Have a wonderful evening.

Presenting a Cheque to a Notable Patron

Tonight's dinner, thanks to your support and to the generosity of our sponsors and donors, will raise several thousands of pounds for a very special cause. A cause fortunate enough to have been enthusiastically embraced by a very special person, our guest of honour, Lady Edith Caulfield.

(Expect applause)

For the benefit of those of you who may not be familiar with the background of our society, you may like to know that it was formed back in 1956 to give the members of our industry regular opportunities to complain to each other about how terrible business was.
The most gratifying tradition to have developed in the last few years has been our connection with 'Child Welfare International'.

We live in a world where children continue to be victims; victims of famine and natural disasters, victims of politics and conflict, victims of ignorance . . . victims of evil.

In fifty different countries, one organization in particular is making a significant difference. Over five million children world-wide are being given comfort and hope through the work of 'CWI'.

What more deserving cause could there possibly be?

Children are the future . . . and we have every reason to rejoice in an organization which recognises this simple truth.
Our industry is proud to play a part in supporting it through functions like this.

So once again, let me thank everybody involved, our members, our sponsors and our donors for their wonderful generosity.

My term as President of this club has just begun and I look forward to a multitude of responsibilities and commitments, many of them – no doubt – 'ABCD' . . . 'above and beyond the call of duty' . . .
Tonight however, I have to perform one of the more pleasant and satisfying functions of a President . . .

Lady Caulfield, it's my pleasure, on behalf of the Federated Services Association, our sponsors and many other generous supporters, to invite you to accept this cheque for £59,000 as our contribution towards the wonderful work which is being done every day by your organization.

I'm sure 'Child Welfare International' will put this money to excellent use.

(present cheque to Lady Caulfield)

. . . and now, some lines – pro *and* anti-charity.

I couldn't decide whether to help Save the Whale, Save the Rain Forests or Save the Children so in the end, I decided to save the money.

Next year we're planning a charity Chinese cookery demonstration . . . a 'Sponsored Wok'!

He sings for charity . . . if you've ever heard him sing, you'll realise he *needs* it!

Imelda Marcos did a lot to help Jewish charities . . . she planted thousands of shoe trees in Israel.

We were put on this earth to help others . . . but why are the others here?

He's a philanthropist . . . mind you, tonight he's more 'pist' than 'philanthro'.

CLICHÉS

I'm tempted to say, 'Avoid clichés like the plague!', but that would be a cheap and facile gag and therefore perfectly suitable for this book.

The real difficulty with clichés is that, by their very nature, they have become so much a part of the language, it's easy to forget they're being used, so at least try to be conscious of them.

Of course, to be fair on these hackneyed phrases, they wouldn't have become clichés had they not been expressive and appropriate in the first place. However, their original meanings have often become obscured and, worse, people get them wrong.

You've heard the expression, 'Laughing all the way to the bank!' Well, you shouldn't have done! The correct phrase is 'Crying all the way to the bank!' So there!

The line seems to have been invented by Liberace and used in his autobiography. He wrote, 'When the reviews are bad, I tell my staff that they can join me as I cry all the way to the bank'.

To fill a speech, or even a conversation, with trite banalities and stereotypical phrases, merely drives people into the clutches of professional writers like me.

So keep it up.

Meanwhile, here are a few sayings that *would* have been clichés if I'd left 'em alone.

Hard work never killed anybody! . . . but then, of course, neither did hanging about.

Life's too short, and so is Danny de Vito!

As Anna-Nicole Smith recently said, 'The bigger they are, the harder they fall'!

A bird in the hand is useless if you want to blow your nose!

Remember – keep a stiff upper lip . . . feel free to do whatever you like with the lower one!

If at first you don't succeed . . . pretend you weren't trying.

CLOSINGS

An awful lot of rubbish is written about the closing of speeches. In most cases, there's really no need for anything particularly clever. Once you've said what you needed to say, you simply shove a full stop at the end of it and get the hell out of there.

People will love you for it.

Of course, you do have to make sure it sounds like you've reached the natural conclusion of your message or messages. If your speech has more than one point to make, it's usually a good idea to run through these issues again just before you finish.

It's advisable to have these headlines all in one place in case you have to break for the border, amigo.

Let me explain.

Too often an audience knows a speech is over before the speaker does. You have to pick up on this before it becomes a problem. Your instinct should tell you that you've done enough.

At that point, go straight to your closing section.

Go directly.

Do not pass 'Go'.

Do not collect £200.

Mark your 'retreat' point very clearly. I always draw a large red star at the top right-hand corner of the page containing the closing section. This ensures it's easy to find, should your audience go cold on you. Once again, however, don't forget to summarise your message within that section.

It can sometimes be fun to end with a bit of mock philosophy, or advice. Occasionally you can use the ending to illustrate or reinforce a point. If, for instance, you'd been advising your audience not to underestimate the competition, you could close like this:

> **I leave you with the famous words of American Civil War General John Sedgwick, who was inspecting his front line troops and was advised by an officer to take cover out of sight of enemy snipers.**
> **Sedgwick scoffed, 'Nonsense', he said, 'they couldn't hit an elephant at this dist . . . '**

In the following lines, I've included a few all-purpose toasts. As closers, these little guys work really well.

> **Here's to happy days . . . any twit can have a good time at night!**

Here's to you, here's to me
May we never disagree.
But if we do, to hell with you
And here's to me!

My horoscope this morning said, 'This is your lucky day – people will be so moved by your words and captivated by your charm and your wit, that they will rise to their feet at the end of your speech in a spontaneous standing ovation'!
Ladies and gentlemen, I leave it to you – do you want to make a liar out of Russell Grant?

Here's champagne to our real friends . . . and real pain to our sham friends.

Now that we've all enjoyed a wonderful meal, I'd like to remind you that wild, uninhibited applause burns up twenty-five calories a minute! . . .
so start burning!
Cheers.

Ladies and gentlemen, I'd like to propose a 'groast' . . . that's a combination of grace and a toast:
'Lord, bless this bunch while they munch lunch'.

Well gentlemen, here's looking at you . . . and, believe me, it's not easy!

I will treasure the memory of tonight until the day I die . . .
or Tuesday, whichever comes first.

In conclusion, ladies and gentlemen, let us have a few moments silence in memory of the fourteen thousand prawns and two hundred chickens, who gave their lives to make this dinner possible!

Finally, I've been asked by the organisers to announce that, for reasons of safety, at the end of this talk, you are requested to refrain from getting up on to the tables or chairs during my standing ovation.
Thank you for your co-operation.
Goodnight.

COMPETITORS

Most responsible companies these days prefer to treat their competitors with a certain amount of gentlemanly respect.

At least in public.

I must warn you, therefore, that some of these lines are quite vicious and would be unsuitable for all but the most crude and ill-mannered. The more professional, sophisticated reader will no doubt wish to skip this section altogether.

Right folks, now that we've got rid of those goody, goody stuck-up bastards, let's get on with it . . .

Do you know how many people work there? . . . about one in four!

You always know where you are with Clomco – They let you down every time.

Their logo ought to be a rhinoceros . . . it's thick-skinned, short-sighted and charges a lot.

Last year Rivaco copied three of Clomco's designs . . .
Now that's a little like stealing the battle plans from General Custer!

It's not for me to say that their prices are too high, but why do they have a showroom *and* a recovery room.

COMPUTERS

Bearing in mind that I'm writing this book on a computer, and that I'm depending on it not to do anything nasty to my work, I've made a deal with my PC that this book will be EC – Electronically Correct.

Computers have feelings too you know.

They're easily offended.

The mere fact that we regularly back-up our work implies an insulting lack of trust. This has become such common practice that the citizens of Cyberworld have become resigned to it. But they don't have to like it.

Anyway, as I have no desire to become the subject of a Pentium Fatwa, I won't be making any computerist jokes.

I certainly don't want to wake up one morning to find that, somehow, my word processor connected itself with my food processor and shredded all my decent gags!

If that happened, I don't think I could bring myself to face the fax.

So I won't be telling you that back in 1966, when the French Foreign Legion bought its very first computer, they immediately programmed it . . . to forget!

I won't be offering any smarty-pants definitions, like:

> **Hardware: where the problem lies according to the software people.**

And . . .

> **Software: where the problem lies according to the hardware people.**

I won't be giving you stuff like:

> **Good news from my last company . . .**
> **The computer that replaced me just fired the bloke who bought it!**

I won't be doing that.

I'm not going to start pointing out that:

> **People in every walk of life are now using computers . . . even TV stars.**
> **For instance, I hear that Pamela Anderson has a top-of-the-range Apple . . .**
> **Mind you, she's also got a first class pear.**

That line is both computerist *and* sexist, so I won't be doing that.

I won't even quote the wise words of humorist Robert Orben who says:

'It is better to be on the Internet than never to have any sex life at all.'

I'd be asking for trouble if I wrote:

It only takes a computer a fraction of a second to make the kind of mistake that would otherwise take a team of experts hundreds of years.

There's another reason you won't find computer jokes between these pages. Technology changes so fast that many of the one-liners could be out of date by the time this book is printed.

As MS-DOS begins to fade into history alongside vinyl records and CB Radio, so does the significance of the once-clever sign hanging above a certain office computer:

'Abandon hope all ye who press enter here.'

(At this rate, I'll end up in a DOS house.)

So no computer jokes.

They're not worth the risk.

Sorry.

CONFERENCES AND MEETINGS

In my experience, it can be a real worry watching a collection of supposedly intelligent executives trying to reach a decision.

Early in the meeting, it could easily take forty-five minutes of meandering discussion to decide upon a print colour for the cover of the Annual Report . . .

Near lunch time, however, a spend of 2.5 million on new plant is approved in two minutes flat.

Honestly, it's enough to make Parkinson wet his pants!

To paraphrase Otto von Bismark, sometimes decisions are very much like sausages . . . it's better not to see them being made.

You can always rely on a Prussian for a side-splitting joke.

This afternoon, I'm happy to say, I find myself surrounded by the most co-operative, warm and enthusiastic bunch of colleagues it's ever been my privilege to creep up to!

**Earlier today, I watched and listened as a new delegate walked over to one of the tables and asked the girl, 'Excuse me, do I register with you?' . . .
'No', she said, 'I'm afraid you're not my type!'**

Some people are saying that if last year's conference is anything to go by, we should let this one go by as well.

At a conference, people get up to speak, say nothing, nobody listens . . . then everyone disagrees.

A productive meeting should function like a think tank . . .
Of course a lot of people believe that a 'think tank' is where a few executives sit around for a bit, think for a bit . . . then get tanked.

Compromise: An arrangement whereby people who can't get what they want, make sure that nobody else does either.

I'm happy to answer your questions as long as you promise not to question my answers . . . this job's tough enough already.

We're now going to be taking a short break . . . it's the second shift.
Those of you who are asleep can now wake up, and those of you who stayed awake . . . it's your turn to take a nap!

Meetings are very important . . . they fill in the spaces between coffee breaks and lunch.

Our board meetings are fascinating.
Actually, we have a very sophisticated system for decision making . . .
You can sum it up in four words . . . 'Eenie, Meenie, Miney, Mo!'

(See also 'Emcee Lines')

THE CORPORATE WIMP

This guy has seen the future . . . and doesn't want to go.

Unfortunately, Terry Holmes can't be with us tonight . . . bit of an accident . . . he was washing David Carter's car and his tongue ran dry!

He's spent so much time buttering up the chairman, he's developed a cholesterol problem!

This man knows no fear . . . ask him to take a risk and he'll say, 'No fear!'

One thing's for sure, in this company, he's the one who makes all the indecisions.

He's spent so much time in the middle of the road that he's got cat's eye burns on his arse!

But he's not a 'Yes Man' . . . when Dave Carter says 'No', *he* says 'No'.

Before Terry attempts to argue with his boss, he makes one hundred per cent sure he's right . . . then he lets the matter drop.

(Flexi line)

He has everything it takes to be a success . . . a quiet charm, a persuasive manner, the ability to grovel without wrinkling his suit!

(Use 'laddering her tights' for the female version.)

On his desk, he has a sign: 'My decision is 'maybe', and that's final!'

He's a man of few words, but then of course, he's married!

Our company likes to hire men with spirit . . . it gives them something to break.

(See also 'Losers')

CUSTOMERS

The customer may not always be right but he's always the one with the money.

The whole idea is to make your customer sit up and take notice . . . unless you're an embalmer.

The pay in the Police Force is good and the hours are reasonable . . . but the best part of the job is that the customer is always wrong!

DEFINITIONS

Comedy is simply a funny way of being serious.

(Peter Ustinov)

After Dinner Speaker: A person who eats a meal they don't want so they can get up and tell a load of stories they can't remember to people who've already heard them.

America: Where they lock up juries and let the defendants out.

Assets: Baby donkeys.

The Big Bang Theory: First there was nothing, then it exploded.

Businessman: Someone who talks golf all morning at the office, and business all afternoon on the golf course!

(Bridging line)

Committee: A group of the unfit, appointed by the unwilling, to do the unnecessary.

Decision: What a man takes when he can't find anybody to serve on a committee.

Economist: A person who guesses wrong, but with confidence.

Gentleman's Agreement: The kind of deal neither party wants to put in writing.

Justice: A decision made in your favour.

Middle Age: Halfway between adolescence and obsolescence.

Music lover: A man who hears a girl singing in the bath and puts his ear to the keyhole.

Opportunist: Someone who made a decision while you were still trying to make up your mind!

'Religion is what keeps the poor from murdering the rich.'

(Napoleon)

Temptation: A ventriloquist at a funeral.

Transistor: A girl who used to be your brother.

EDUCATION

No wonder we have educational problems in this country; fifty per cent of the population can't read, fifty per cent can't write and the other fifty per cent can't add up!

Terrible scandal at Roedene . . . they caught one of the girls with a record player in her room . . .
That Chris Evans *really* gets around!

So many kids these days are subjected to questionable influences and bad company . . . but then, you can hardly stop them mixing with their own parents, can you?

He says he'll never understand metrication if he lives to be a gross!

Some of his fellow students at University later became lawyers and politicians . . . others became useful members of society.

(Bridging line) (Flexi line)

All this talk about dyslexia . . . I don't even believe the condition exists. I think it's a load of carp!

When he was seventeen, his father sent him abroad to study.
Wow! He certainly learned a few things from her!

EGO

I'm very fond of Nick Webster, but not as much as *he* is . . .

Wasn't it Nick who said, 'There but for the grace of me, goes God!'?

Over the years, he's been such an asset to the company, that I really felt I had to mention him . . . and so did he!

Actually, ladies and gentlemen, Nick Webster couldn't make it tonight . . . but you may just be able to pick out his ego floating above the top table.

He's not very well this evening.
He's suffering from an impacted love bite . . .
self-inflicted, of course.

What can you say about a man who calls 'Dial-A-Prayer'
every day to see if he has any messages?

What a poser! I'd wring his neck, but it's probably ex-
directory!

It's not easy for me to pay tribute to this man . . . he
does it so much better himself.

There have been many great love stories in history . . .
Abélard and Héloïse, Romeo and Juliet, King Edward
VIII and Mrs Simpson, Nick Webster and Nick
Webster.

In his office, there are loads of photographs of him
plastered all over one wall . . .
On the other wall, there are photos of him sober.

(Bridging line)

His prized possession is on his desk, inscribed, 'To
the greatest guy I know!' . . . and, let me tell you, I've
never seen a mirror so well polished!

He came into the office and said, 'How's my favourite
guy doing today?'
I said, 'You look fine to me'.

But he's a thoughtful man. In his will, he's leaving his

house to his wife, his money to his children and his ego to Brian Clough.

His great uncle Albert Webster was a contortionist ... he was a sad and lonely man. At the age of seventy-five, he had a heart attack and died in his own arms.

This man is totally self-sufficient ... his love life could be described as a 'ménage à moi'!

He's talented, charming, intelligent, witty and handsome.
In fact, he reminds me of *me*!

EMCEE LINES

When acting as Master of Ceremonies (MC) at a conference or a seminar, don't be too lavish or long-winded with your introductions. Even if you know the speaker to be good, he or she may be having an 'off' day. In any case, building the speechmaker up too much could disappoint the audience if the speaker can't deliver.

Introduce and back-announce the speakers, listen to the points made in each presentation and, at the end, say something which proves you've heard it.

(If you can sound like you've actually understood it, that's even better.)

Most of the following one-liners are *fun*-liners. Be careful not to belittle a speaker unless it's appropriate, totally in character with the occasion, and clear to all that you don't really mean a word of it.

Many of these gags are interchangeable with those under 'Roast Lines'.

Our next speaker has been called the most creative and influential in his field, and who am I to disagree with his mother?

This man could be described as charming, intelligent and entertaining . . . and perhaps one day, he *will* be!

I must say those comments covered a wide field . . . I don't know what they covered the field *with*, but I'm sure next year we're going to have a bumper harvest!

Laugh and the world laughs with you.
Frown . . . and you're probably thinking of . . . Stan Pearce.

Stop beating about the bush! If you have anything to say, shut up!

An extra item . . . a little later we're going to be hearing from the treasurer . . . and his accomplices.

Now I think we'll take Stan Pearce . . . and I think we'll leave him there.

You can normally rely on Stan for rather outrageous material . . . tonight, it seems to be his shirt!

(Bridging line)

Witty, charming, intelligent . . . as he's been described in failed lie detector tests!

I could really listen to him speak all night, and for a time there I thought I was going to have to!

I'm told his speech is going to be quite serious . . . there won't be any jokes.
Of course, with a suit like that, who needs jokes?

(Bridging line)

You know, people warned me that it would be difficult to follow a speech by Trevor Richards, and they were quite right . . . I couldn't follow a bloody word of it!

(See also 'Replying')

EXECUTIVES

They say that the trouble with business life these days is that there are too many one-ulcer men holding down two-ulcer jobs.

That's what 'they' say.

As soon as I find out who 'they' are, I'll have to send them a few quid for the gag.

A shrewd executive recruits optimists as sales staff and pessimists as credit controllers.
You can always spot a good sales director . . .
he has a worried look on his sales manager's face!

A top executive is a man who has the luxury of taking as long as he wants . . . to make a snap decision.

Some people say that the Board of Directors and Stonehenge have a lot in common . . . they're old, they don't move and nobody is certain how they came to be in that position.

(Flexi line)

An executive is someone who slows down production by asking employees for reports on why production is down.

He's a fine go-ahead executive . . . ask him any old crap and he'll say, 'Fine, go ahead!'

A lot of people believe that on our board, half the directors do the work and the other half do nothing.
Well, as a matter of fact, it's just the reverse.

A successful executive knows exactly how to delegate all the responsibility, shift all the blame and grab all the credit.

EXPERTS AND CONSULTANTS

The late Malcolm S. Forbes once said:

What's an expert? I read somewhere that the more a man knows, the more he knows he doesn't know. So I suppose one definition of an expert would be someone who doesn't admit out loud that he knows enough about a subject to know he doesn't really know much.'

Mind you, Malcolm Forbes also said, 'These pink leotards are getting much too tight!', so you can't go by him.

Listen to me, reader old son, *I'll* tell you what an expert is . . .
'ex' is a has-been, and 'spurt' is a drip under pressure.

A consultant is someone who can save his client almost enough to pay his fee.

Did you hear about the business efficiency expert who put unbreakable glass in all the fire alarms?

What this company needs today is . . . fewer experts on what this company needs today.

An expert can take something you already knew, and make it sound totally confusing.

How's this for a contradiction? 'The experts disagree.'

Expert opinion is subjective. Don't rely on it.
If you ask a chicken how a chicken should be stuffed, it'll say, 'Worms, seeds and beetles'.

An expert knows all the answers . . . but only if you ask all the right questions.

A financial adviser is a person who can tell you what to do with your money after you've already done something else with it!

Last month we had our office cat neutered . . . he still hangs around at night with the other cats, but now he's just a consultant.

(See also 'Advice')

FILTH AND NAUGHTINESS

There's absolutely no place in this book for smut and vulgarity.

Except here.

Some of the language I use in these one-liners will not always be suitable for every occasion. Feel free to moderate the expletives but bear in mind that some lines actually depend on a rude word for maximum impact – that element of naughtiness gives the line an extra humorous edge.

Not always, but more often than you'd think.

As an example, take these two definitions:

• **'The ideal legal client is a very wealthy man in deep shit!'**

• **'The ideal legal client is a very wealthy man in a great deal of trouble!'**

The first version will produce a belly laugh, the second will bring forth a genial, knowing giggle.

Nevertheless, by changing the 'deep shit' ending, the line has not been killed. It's still worth using. You just have to accept that by toning down the language you've toned down the reaction.

There are, of course, all sorts of substitutions you could use but please be aware that certain one-liners are useless without the ripe language – they lack a certain vital eloquence.

Some years ago, when a famous recording star turned down one of my songs on the grounds that he didn't believe it would sell, I could easily have shrugged it off like a good sport and thanked him for listening. But just imagine how much more impact was created by the colourful observation I actually made at the time, namely, 'You wouldn't know a hit song if it flew up your arse and bit your liver!'

Cliff turned to religion shortly afterwards.

Use the following lines with great care – even at stag events – and don't inject this kind of material into your speech just because it shocks.

That's a desperate cop out.

> **The way words sound can sometimes be quite misleading . . .**
> **For instance, a seminar has nothing to do with semen . . . it's a mass debate.**

Statistics can be fascinating . . . for instance, according to a recent 'Cosmopolitan' survey, twenty-four per cent of women, when asked if they'd ever faked an orgasm, answered, 'Yes! yes! Oh my God, yes!'

(Bridging line)

I've always been amused at the way technocrats adore acronyms . . . RAM, ROM, DOS, ASCII.
Well, I might as well admit it . . . I come under a special category . . . 'Can't-Understand-New-Technology' . . . and if anybody suggests using an acronym for that, they're in big trouble!

(Henry Fletcher)

Make that decision . . . to hell with the bull . . . take *yourself* by the horn!

Our next guest is about as welcome as a piranha in a bidet.

This guy's really in trouble . . . he's even overdrawn at the sperm bank!

He's a lucky bastard . . . he has the body of a twenty year old . . . about twice a week!

He's a mixture of paranoia and apathy . . .
He knows they're out to get him, but he doesn't give a shit!

I know I shouldn't comment on his physical dimensions, but he went to a hooker once and she charged him a finder's fee!

Channel Four is doing a documentary about his sex life . . . it's called '60 Seconds'.

GOLF AND OTHER SPORTS

Corporate golf days, followed by dinner in the club house, can be most conducive to cordial business relations.

I'm sure you don't need me to tell you that your speech should avoid placing too much emphasis on business matters; your customers must not be made to feel like hostages to your hospitality. Stick to the social aspects of the occasion, and allow your guests to absorb your corporate character on a subliminal level.

Anything less subtle could be counter-productive.

Of course, if you choose your lines cleverly, bridging them into business-related topics, or correlating sporting issues with corporate strategy, you'll be admired and warmly received.

Don't linger on company matters, keep the topics moving and be super-cool.

Just like me, mate.

Ladies and gentlemen, I don't propose to beat around the bush this evening . . .
We had quite enough of that out on the course today.

Ah yes, give me some golf clubs, some fresh air, and a beautiful woman . . . and you can *keep* the bloody clubs and the fresh air!

(Flexi line)

Actually, I don't play a lot of golf these days. I prefer sex . . . it's much more fun and you don't need a caddie to tell you which stick to use!

(Bridging line)

Cricket's good too. In cricket, when you hit a ball into the grandstand, you just forget about it . . . in golf, you have to go *looking* for the bloody thing!

My youngest son makes a perfect caddie . . . he's strong, he's dependable and he's unable to count past ten.

Ladies and gentlemen, in my opinion, it's impossible to praise Bob Graham's golfing abilities too highly . . . it's impossible to praise them at all . . . he's crap!

(Flexi line)

Mind you, he's never lost a ball . . . he's never hit it *far* enough to lose it!

His vicar told him that playing golf is a sin.
He said, 'Do you mean on a Sunday? . . .
The vicar said, 'No, *any* day . . . I've seen you play!'

He's spent so much time in the sand, they've made him an honorary colonel in the French Foreign Legion!

By the way, Bruce Turner apologises . . . he can't be here tonight.
He's been suffering from his old sports injury, 'Racecourse Pocket'.

(Bridging line)

So tonight he'll be badly missed . . . badly missed, just like a typical Bob Graham shot!

That guy drives me nuts on the course.
He keeps shouting, 'Fore! . . . Fore! . . . Fore!'
. . . and that's only when he's putting!

Bob *thinks* he's good at golf . . .
probably because he gets to hit the ball much more often than anyone else!

He's a good loser, but then of course, he's had a lot of practice.

At least his job is totally secure . . . he was the only person playing golf with the boss the day he got his hole in one!

(Bridging line)

Harry Fisher is one *hell* of a sportsman. Only recently he successfully combined two sports . . . hurdles and cricket!
He jumped bail!

(Bridging line)

The trouble with being a good sport is that you have to *lose* to prove it.

I do fifty push ups nearly every day . . . not intentionally – I just fall down a lot!

(Bridging line)

Actually, I quite enjoy jogging . . . it's just that long ambulance ride home that gets to me.

Footballers are such wimps . . . yesterday, one player was injured during the coin toss!

Our team is very similar to an old-fashioned bra . . . no cups and poor support!

Their goalie missed such an easy save that in despair, he put his head in his hands . . . and missed that too!

None of the Fulham players is allowed to own a dog. There's a very good reason for that . . . they can't hold on to a lead!

There are two kinds of football teams in this country: those who fired their managers before the season started, and those who *wish* they had.

What a player! He put the ball straight into the net every time.
Trouble was, he was playing tennis!

(Bridging line)

I told her I was a little stiff from rugby.
She said, 'It doesn't matter where you come from, it's what's inside your heart that matters'.

Rugby is like sex . . . you don't have to be good at it to enjoy it.

(Flexi line)

Jimmy Burns is very keen on rugby. Of course, these days, he doesn't actually *play* it, but when he goes to an England match, out of respect he always wears a jock strap . . .
Doesn't he know you're supposed to wear them on the *inside* of your trousers?!

Skiing is a wonderful sport. It consists of wearing fourteen hundred quids worth of clothes and equipment, then flying eight hundred miles in order to stand around in a bar and get pissed.

GREEN ISSUES AND RECYCLED TISSUES

Help save the rainforest . . . shoot a woodpecker!

He's so environmentally-friendly, he uses unleaded petrol in his Zippo!

Global warming . . . a terrible thing!
Men get it if they sit in a bath that's too hot!

Thanks to science, at least we know the earth is not flat . . . yet!

If you want a breath of fresh air in Los Angeles, you have to step *in*side!

Trendy local councils are beginning to employ non-orthodox contractors . . .
Goodearth District Authority have taken on an aromatherapist to work with local sewage engineers.

It gets worse. Down the road at Greentown, the Transport Department are employing an alternative maintenance engineer . . . he uses acupuncture to repair tyres.

Whose idea was it to publish and distribute fourteen million leaflets saying, 'Save Paper'?

He's environmentally confused . . . he talks to plants. The plant at Sellafield, the plant at Heysham, the plant at Humberside . . .

Good planets are hard to find . . . let's try to keep this one in decent shape.

GRUNGE AND GUCCI

He:
Robin Morgan dresses outrageously because he's not happy with himself . . . and I think he's right.

That jacket looks like something Marks made when Spencer wasn't looking.

Yes, Robin's taste in clothes *is* rather bizarre.
To give you some idea, one day last month, a moth flew into his wardrobe . . . and threw up!

Hi Robin . . . that's quite a suit . . .
Nice of Coco The Clown to remember you in his will.

Let's not be too hard on him . . . it's not easy being a slave to fashion when one head is missing off your bunny slippers!!

Ladies and gentlemen, a rare sight – a Conservative in a Socialist suit!

(Bridging line)

But he's really made the effort this evening – he's immaculate! If he dropped dead tonight, they wouldn't have to do a thing at the funeral parlour!

That suit he's wearing is a fashion statement . . .
It's saying, 'He can't really afford to wear me'.

Mind you, he's a generous man. I'll never forget the time he surprised his wife with a mink coat . . .
she'd never seen him wearing one before!

She:

Marion Stacey has had many men in her life – Giorgio Armani, Gianni Versace, Yves Saint Laurent . . .

Marion's a born-again Christian Dior.

By the way, the gown she's wearing tonight is a Paris creation . . .
Mind you, so was the Guillotine!

I personally think she's getting too thin . . . last week she had a run in her stockings and her left leg fell out!

HAS-BEENS AND ZIMMER-SURFERS

We're paying tribute today to one of the best salesmen of the decade . . . the 1930s.

A man who has a wonderful future behind him.

A man who still signs his contracts with a quill!

A man who has spent thirty-five years, riding along on the crest of a slump.

This guy goes way back.
He was working here long before the new technology. In those days, the only office copier . . . was a monk!

He swears by potatoes to make him look younger . . . he doesn't eat them; he *mashes* them and uses them to grout his wrinkles!

At his age, the best part of waking up in the morning . . . is . . . waking up in the morning!

This is a man who doesn't have an enemy in the world . . . they're all dead.

He's worth a fortune . . . he *must* be . . . he's got silver in his hair, gold in his teeth, rare stones in his kidneys, lead in his feet . . . and gas in his stomach!

HE'S BEEN AROUND SO LONG . . .

He can remember when the Archers only had an allotment.

He can remember when the Dead Sea was still alive.

He can remember when rainbows only came in black and white.

He can remember when Heinz had only one variety.

He can remember when Madame Butterfly was just a caterpillar.

He can remember when doctors made home deliveries, and pizza restaurants didn't.

HECKLING

I caused a bit of a scene once at a meeting, when I described a fellow director's pompous outburst as a 'Cri d'arse'.

To this day, I'm not really sure whether that made me the heckler or the hecklee.

Either way, I thought I deserved a round of applause.

Night club comics often have to cope with loudmouth drunks and various nasty customers. The comedian is usually well-armed with several lines designed to turn the tables on the smart-arse and to get an extra laugh or two at the heckler's expense.

At a business event, however, you're most unlikely to be faced with this kind of interruption. Even at a corporate social gathering, any heckling is usually very good-natured and restrained.

It would be rather heavy-handed, if not churlish, for a speaker like you to learn professional anti-heckler lines simply for the purpose of silencing someone who is simply enjoying the evening.

So here they are . . .

What a strange way of giving in your notice.

Hey you, belt up! When I want your opinion I'll call your wife.

I'd ask for the results of your IQ test, but I'm sure fractions don't count.

You know, you really shouldn't drink on an empty head!

Now *there's* a gentleman with a ready wit . . .
(turn to heckler)
    let me know when it's ready.
(more than one heckler?)
    Ah, Doctor Heckle and Mr Snide.

What's on your mind? . . . If you'll excuse the overstatement.

I'd like you to meet my co-star . . .
(point to heckler)

Feel free to speak your mind . . . I have a spare three seconds!

It's so wonderful to be in front of my own kind of people . . . *piss artists*!

Hi there! And you certainly are!

Nice to see your voice is working . . . shame it's not connected to anything.

Isn't she a treasure? I wonder who dug her up.

Hey! I thought alcoholics were meant to be anonymous!

Is there a new life-form out there that we don't yet know about?

Oh well, every village has one.

Would you mind closing the door for me please? . . . from the outside!

INTERNATIONAL AFFAIRS

A few years ago, I was part of a gathering hosted by President and Mrs Clinton at the White House in Washington.

Bill Clinton made a short welcoming speech. It was simple and rather eloquent.

The style was, I thought, deliberately reminicent of his hero, Jack Kennedy.

President Kennedy's criteria for preparing speeches was always 'audience comprehension and comfort':

- Short speeches made with short words.

- A logical sequence of points.

- Sentences, phrases and paragraphs constructed in order to simplify, emphasise and illuminate.

No speech ran longer than twenty to thirty minutes and Kennedy wasted no words and no time.

For his openings, he usually used humour to establish a rapport with his audience and later, in the body of the speech, he used historical illustrations and quotations in order to highlight important points.

He was also fond of soundbites like 'Ich bin ein Berliner'.

I've always wondered what he'd have said in Hamburg.

Everybody's talking about trading relations with the countries of the former Eastern Bloc.
I'm all for it! . . . They can have my brother-in-law for a start!

Another former Soviet republic has defied Russia and adopted a fiercely independent stance.
They've held a referendum and the people have made their choice . . .
they're going with Burger King!

I can tell you that England lost a very special man when Richard went over to run our operation in Gibraltar.
Even today, hundreds of people are calling for him to return to London . . . hundreds of people in Gibraltar.

Incidentally, a very warm welcome to the representatives from the Association of Paper Napkin Workers: The Serviette Union!

Andorra . . . now *there's* a small country. I tried calling it last week and got their answering machine.

It's such a small country, the National Anthem only has one note: 'Laaaaah!'
well . . . show some respect – stand up!

Question: How many Dutchmen does it take to change a tulip bulb?

Question: Why do the Swiss keep the best part of the cheese for themselves?

You can't always draw simple parallels. For instance, just because Swiss cheese is full of holes doesn't necessarily mean they can't make perfectly good condoms.

Steve Weston can't be with us today. Sadly, he's in a disturbed and confused state . . . California!

Signpost in Mississippi:
'We shoot every third salesman. The second just left!'

The United States' money-supply is getting tighter all the time . . .
It's got so bad that Johnny Cash has changed his name to Johnny Credit!

The Japanese think the English are lazy.
Oh yeah? . . . At least we're not too lazy to cook our fish!

I'll never forget that Yugoslavian girl who hid me in her cellar during the seige of Sarajevo.
As it happens, I was in no real danger – she was living in Wimbledon at the time.

The plane stops so many times en route to Australia, they ought to change the name of the airline to 'Qantas interruptus'!

Ireland: the only country in the world where 'forty' rhymes with 'thirty'.

The volatile situation in China is constantly on everyone's mind, but there's no reason to be obsessed with it, is there ladies and Tiananmen? . . . uh . . . gentlemen?

Jan Hulsman is very proud of his heritage – he once told me, 'I was born a Belgian, I have lived as a Belgian, and I shall die a Belgian!' . . .
That's the trouble with Jan . . . no ambition!

(Flexi line)

Kurt Scheer is the man who once said to Marcel Marceau, 'We haff ways of making you talk!'

Georgi is from Albania. Not only can he *read* the bottom line of an eye-testing chart . . . this guy can *pronounce* it!

(Flexi line)

He's got a great sideline; he's the one who exports all those American flags the Iranians have been burning.

(See also 'Politics')

INVESTMENTS

How do you ensure success in the equity markets?
According to Will Rogers, it's simple:
'Buy some good stock. Hold it till it goes up . . . and then sell it.
If it doesn't go up, don't buy it!'

Take a positive view of the stock market. Say to yourself:
'Today is the first day of the rest of my money!'

I always seem to choose the 'Sweet Chariot' shares ...
As soon as I buy them, they swing low!

Actually, I have an enormous portfolio of Penny Shares ...
Mind you, they weren't that way when I first bought 'em!

I lost a hell of a lot of money because of Lloyds, but from that experience I grew ... I grew tense, I grew irritable, I grew depressed ... I grew ulcers.

The bible says, 'We brought nothing into this world, and it is certain we can carry nothing out'.
So, in a sense, Lloyds of London was only doing the Lord's work!

THE JOB

As long as the context and the atmosphere of your speech makes it clear that you are only kidding, there's nothing wrong with complaining about your job. It's a very English thing to do. You could, of course, use certain lines in this section to criticise your *previous* job and contrast that with your current position, which, if you're that much of a wimp, is obviously bloody desperate.

I'm not very impressed with reincarnation . . . I had this bloody job *last* time!

Every Friday I used to take my salary to the bank . . . I *had* to take it – it was too little to go by itself!

My job here is very much like being a mushroom . . . they keep me in the dark, they pile on the crap and any day now they'll probably have me canned!

People say that any idiot could do this job.
Honestly, that's stupid! . . . I can tell you, there's a helluva lot more to doing this job than just being an idiot!

There are two things I love about this job . . . Saturdays and Sundays!

At one time I *was* going to be a priest but I kept giggling during the Last Rites!

This business is fickle . . . one minute you're called 'outstanding', next minute, that's where you are and that's where you're standing.

Why do I work? I work for a good cause . . . *cause* I need the money.

While I was working there, I gradually learned to appreciate the little things in life . . . like my salary.

Around the office, he's a real go-getter . . . coffee, mostly!

There's just no job security these days . . . my option comes up every thirty minutes!

LAWYERS AND THE LAW

Lawyers are fair game; everybody loves to hate 'em.
We tend to place them in the same category as Tax Inspectors, Gutter Journalists, Estate Agents and Serial Killers.

However, let's not confuse the average shyster with somebody who *gives* a bugger.

After all, why should he?
Firstly, he's incredibly thick-skinned. Secondly, he'll always win, whatever happens.

Well, reader old son, it's time to declare 'Open Season' for these people . . . so go get the bastards!

Here's my advice: next time your lawyer tries to charge you an arm and a leg . . . give him the finger!

(Flexi line)

Accusing a lawyer of being unscrupulous is a bit like accusing a hooker of sleeping around.

The ideal legal client is a very wealthy man in deep shit.

What do Sherlock Holmes, Daffy Duck and an honest lawyer have in common? They're all fictitious characters.

(Flexi line)

Ninety per cent of all lawyers give the other ten per cent a bad name.

(Flexi line)

A lawyer is a man who encourages two other men to strip for a fight, and then runs off with their clothes!

Question: What's brown and black and looks good on a lawyer?
Answer: A rottweiler!

(Flexi line)

I once had a little talking bird that used to lie under oath . . .
A perjurygar!

A legal adviser is someone who has the expertise to explain a problem you didn't know you had, in a way you can't understand.

When Gerry Marshall did some legal work for us last year, he sent us a bill for £63,000!
Of course it was a computer error and when I 'phoned him, he said, 'Don't worry . . . just go ahead and pay it . . . I'll deduct it from your next bill!'

When I complained how much he was charging me, he said, 'You're so ungrateful! . . . and to think I named my yacht after you!'

In school, Gerry was voted 'The boy most likely to settle out of court'.

Let's face it, this guy's forgotten more about the law than he ever knew!

Gerry and Julia don't have much in common . . . he's a lawyer and she's a human being.

But lawyers are very important . . . think how boring the world would be if everything was as simple as it really is!

Everybody involved in a court case – defence, prosecution, expert witnesses, defendants – manipulate the facts to support their position.
Our whole legal system is based on the premise that if everybody lies, the truth will come out!
In other words, the best liar is deemed to be telling the truth!

I once had this big dispute over a leather jacket.
The shop said it was leather and I said it was vinyl.
So we went to arbitration where the judge's decision was vinyl.

Corny? . . . So sue me!

LAZY

His parents were hard working people. They used to get up every morning at 5.30, do sixteen hours of strenuous work and thought nothing of it.
He's the same way . . . he doesn't think much of it either.

He's not lazy exactly; it's just that he likes to relax over a cup of coffee . . . sometimes for three or four months.

He has a positive attitude towards work . . . he positively doesn't want to do any!

The trouble with doing nothing all the time is . . . how do you know when you're finished?

He was never the type to sit watching the clock, waiting for half-past-five . . . he used to leave at four!

He was a model salesman . . . unfortunately he wasn't a working model.

He likes having his work cut out for him . . . entirely.

To this man, hard work is second nature. Unfortunately, *first* nature is . . . buggering about!

What devotion! . . . he thinks nothing of working twenty-four hours a week!

Back in the Sixties, when everybody else tuned in, turned on and dropped out, he used to tune out, turn in and drop off!

LOSERS

If you are going to make 'loser' jokes at someone else's expense, make sure your victim has broad shoulders and that the lines you use are carefully chosen and pitched just right.

These lines are also effective when made at your own expense. Should you wish to demonstrate that you don't take yourself too seriously, the use of self-deprecating humour can be quite endearing.

So be my guest . . .
Go ahead and deprecate all over yourself.

> **Life has its ups and downs you know**
> **That's Nature's wicked rub**
> **So if at first you don't succeed,**
> **Welcome to the club!**
>
> (Too modest to attribute)

> **Here I am . . . a squashed hedgehog on the highway of life.**

> **Unlucky? . . . If I went into the funeral business, people would stop dying!**

> **Some guys are really 'with it' . . . I'm nowhere near it.**

> **I suppose it runs in the family. I remember my uncle used to say:**
> **'Mitch my boy . . . life is a parade!'**
> **. . . poor old bastard got run over by a float!**

I simply have no luck. I once asked my local librarian to trace my roots . . . she discovered that my great grandfather had an overdue book, and made me pay the fine!

Bernie McGill gets no respect . . . when he 'phoned the Samaritans, they put him on hold.

That's right, he gets niento respecto . . . last week, when he went in to a client's office, the customer buzzed her secretary and said, 'I'll take all calls! . . . any calls at all'.

Bernie is a man who started his career at the bottom . . . and stayed there!

He's not even worth the paper it took to work out what he was worth on paper!

He's done nothing! Never been arrested, never smoked dope, never been to a whorehouse . . .
For God's sake Bernie, get a *past!*

He's been very depressed about his bypass . . . there was a promotion going in March and he was bypassed!
(Bridging line)

But this man doesn't know the meaning of the word 'quit'. 'Fired' – yes, 'quit' – no.

He has a terrible identity problem . . . he's the only man I know who's listed in *Who's Who* as 'Occupant'!

He has no luck with women . . . when he 'phoned an 0891 sex line, the girl said, 'Not tonight dear, I've got an earache!'

No luck with women at all . . . even Tammy Wynette wouldn't stand by him.

MEAN AND TIGHTFISTED

Letter to the editor of The Times:

Dear Sir,
For some time now, you have been depicting Scottish people as stingy and tightfisted.
This stereotypical cliché is demeaning and insulting to those of us who live North of the Border.
If you continue to publish such offensive and misleading nonsense, I shall have no alternative but to stop borrowing your newspaper!

Yours truly,
Angus McPherson.

When it comes to charity, he gives till it hurts . . . unfortunately, 'hurt' clicks in at about three quid.
(Bridging line)

He's half-Scottish, half-Italian . . . when he's not pinching pennies, he's pinching bottoms!

This guy gives 'frugal' a bad name.
Who else would try to get extra Air Miles by riding round on the airport luggage carousel?

He's so tight, he goes to a discount manicurist and get his nails *bitten*.

He has over three hundred books, but he doesn't have a bookshelf . . . nobody will *lend* him a bookshelf!

For his daughter's tenth birthday, he bought half a cake with five candles and held it in front of a mirror!

He saved himself a lot of money last Christmas by telling the kids that Santa Claus was doing time.

THE MEDIA

Some people are born great, some achieve greatness and some have to hire Max Clifford.

You may think your sex life is good . . . but would you want Barry Norman to do a review on it?

Not everything you read in the papers is Gospel . . .
I mean, Matthew, Mark, Luke and John don't work for *The Sun*.

Hell hath no fury like a tabloid scorned.

Remember, there's one good thing about silence . . . it can't be quoted.

It's a bit much when the only stuff in the newspapers you can rely on being true, are the advertisements!

The secret of success in Television: you have to start at the bottom . . . and kiss it.

(Flexi line)

That show was so bad, the canned audience booed!

(See also 'Advertising')

MEDICAL ISSUES

Scientists in Baltimore have announced that they can now take the DNA from just one tiny piece of tissue, and clone an entire box of Kleenex!

Modern medicine has made great strides; it's progressed from not being able to cure the common cold . . . to not being able to cure AIDS!

Doctors now believe that if a man leads the life-style of a lorry driver, he's at greater risk of becoming HGV positive.

These days, doctors say that sex is perfectly all right after a heart attack . . . provided you close the ambulance door to stop yourself falling out!

Like Michael Douglas, I'm addicted to sex, and I really need some therapy . . .
Not so I can quit – so I can keep *up* with it!

I'm half-Jewish and believe me, it's a *very* strange sight.

Things you don't want to hear during your vasectomy operation:
Number One: The word 'Whoops!'
Number Two: 'Is it left over right or right over left for a reef knot?'
Number Three: 'That reminds me, I must pick up one of those little red chilli peppers on the way home.'

What a doctor! . . . if ever you're at death's door, *he's* the one who'll pull you through!

What a doctor! . . . if you've got trouble with your heartbeat, he'll soon put a stop to it.

MONEY, BANKS AND BANKERS

His fielding experience as a cricketer came in handy for his work at the bank . . . they paid him to try and catch the cheques before the first bounce.

(Bridging line)

A bank is a place where you can keep the government's money until the Inland Revenue asks for it.

(Bridging line)

The reason money doesn't grow on trees? . . . The banks own all the branches.

A couple caught dealing 'soft' drugs in Keswick, deposited the proceeds in a joint account.

I've had a personal domestic problem . . . the contents of my wallet left me for another bank!

I have something Richard Branson *hasn't* got . . . no money!

People in the world of banking are telling us that, with the forthcoming introduction of the new personal smart cards, we're heading for a cashless society.
Hey, that puts me ahead of the game . . . I'm cashless right now!

I like to borrow a little money every month and put it aside for a rainy day.

I hear that a burglar broke into one of the High Street Banks and was incredibly lucky . . . he managed to escape without having to buy an insurance policy!

I spend loads of money on food . . . my family won't eat anything else.

I don't want to say that the company has had a financial disaster, but I can report that Lloyds Bank just set up a field-headquarters in their car park . . . with nurses, blankets, mugs of hot tea . . .

US President Herbert Hoover once said something like:

'Inflation means that as soon as you find you can make ends meet, someone moves the ends.'

Other definitions of inflation abound . . .

Inflation is when you order a fillet steak costing twenty-five pounds, put it on your Visa Card, and it fits!

Inflation . . . where the buck doesn't stop anywhere.

Inflation is when you have money to burn but can't afford the match to light it.

I hate inflation . . . a pound isn't worth twopence anymore!

Honest, it makes you want to spit!

No sooner had I completed my list of witty comments, than some interfering bloody Chancellor started to get both prices and the money supply under control and inflation was no longer an issue.

You know, there's something weirdly inappropriate about a government fighting inflation; somehow it's like the Mafia fighting crime.

Never mind, let's look on the bright side — it's *bound* to be with us again before too long, so hang on to those one-liners.

You'll need 'em.

OPENERS

Coming up are a few lines designed to loosen the collars, set the mood and begin the action.

On nearly every occasion, a good opening is crucial. It's the speaker's way of saying, 'Don't worry folks, this speech is not going to be as boring as you thought'.

Some of the finest speechmakers like to open with an anecdote. An anecdote can be an ideal link into the theme of your presentation. If chosen carefully, a good opening story will illustrate your topic or indicate exactly where you stand on a subject. In short, an effective anecdote is an excellent way to launch a business speech.

I only wish I could think of one for you.

Anecdotes are not really the function of this book. In any case, unless you're a natural raconteur, they are not without risk – especially when used at the very beginning of a speech.

There's really no shortage of books packed with amusing stories suitable for speechmakers. One-liners, on the other hand, are like gold dust. So be thankful.

Here come the openers:

Mr President, Madam Chairman, members of the association, honoured guests, ladies and gentlemen... thirteen words into the speech and *still* no laughs! I must be slipping!

For the benefit of our honoured guests, let me introduce myself; my name is Robert Handley... I'm here to help you through your after-dinner nap.

I've been asked not to bore you with a long speech this afternoon ... so I'm going to have to try my best to bore you with a *short* one. Oh ... and if you want to get away quickly, you can help by laughing fast, all right?

I'm your Master of Ceremonies for the evening, and frankly, there's not an awful lot you can *do* about that.

I have some good news and some bad news.
First, the bad news – after writing and re-writing, editing and re-editing, the very *shortest* I could make this speech run for, was thirty-seven minutes!
That was the bad news ... now for the good news – I was *lying* about the bad news.

Actually, I've been asked to speak no longer than three minutes. Three minutes! ... I normally need more than that just for applause!

They tell me your organization has been searching for a speaker capable of charming you with his spectacular wit, his staggering charisma and his dazzling personality.
Well ... I'm here to fill in while the search continues.

Ladies and gentlemen, and any *lawyers* in the audience ...

(Flexi line)

I've been asked to say a few words because . . . well, the staff want to get home early and they figured that if I made a speech it would be the quickest way to clear the room.

In a large hall . . .

For those of you at the back, if you can't see me properly, I'm tall, dark and look very much like Pierce Brosnan. For those of you at the front . . . please don't tell the ones at the back.

Mr President, members of the committee, fellow associates, colleagues, honoured guests, my lords, ladies and gentlemen . . . well, that's the hardest bit out the way.

As they tell their speakers at Shell . . . if you don't strike oil in three minutes, stop boring!

Ladies and gentlemen, many years ago, when I was a prisoner of war in Vietnam . . . is an excellent way for an accountant to open a speech.
It's a load of crap, but it's an excellent way to open a speech.

(I nearly put this next one in the 'Filth' section, but my worse nature got the better of me.)

The title of my speech today is . . .
'The penis: mightier than the sword.'
(Hastily look at your notes)
Oh sorry! – 'The *pen is* mightier than the sword.'

OVERWEIGHT

Some people are quite comfortable about being overweight; usually the ones who are very fat indeed. Make jokes about fat folks *only* if you're sure they won't be embarrassed or upset. Remember, people are allowed to make jokes against themselves, but this doesn't automatically give *you* the right to do the same thing.

On the other hand, if they're that fat, they probably can't catch you anyway.

Later in this book, under 'Roasts and Insults', I'll be explaining the importance of *truth* in humour.

Your audience has to see or think of your victim as being quite tubby, otherwise the jokes won't work. The extent of his corpulence will control the type of one-liners suitable for use. As you read them, you'll see that some of them imply vastness while others are quite mild in their satire.

One more thing . . . don't use 'fat' jokes against women.

Not even the one that goes:

She's always complaining about her cellulite. I don't see why she doesn't just get cable?

And *certainly* not the one that goes:

Talk about cellulite – one day a blind man tried to read her arse!

These one-liners are vulgar and offensive and you're not allowed to use them.

In fact, you're very naughty for forcing me to print them.

Although I don't intend to make this a long speech, I think it would be useful for me to give you a couple of highlights from the life of our Guest of Honour ... just a potted version ... you know, something consistent with his belly.

This man is not only larger than life, he's also larger than his own trousers!

I must say I'm delighted to see that Phil has made a complete recovery from his anorexia.

I don't want to say he's fat ... but I will! – he's fat!
(Flexi line)

The first time I met Phil Gorman, he was standing on the corner of Oxford Street ... and High Street, Kensington.

Some people dress up as Elvis Presley ... Phil Gorman impersonates *Graceland*!

They say that no man is an island ... let's face it, Phil Gorman comes pretty close.

He's certainly a big eater ... who else do you know who owns a wide-screen microwave?

When he was a kid, he couldn't play 'Hide and Seek'
. . . he was so tubby, all he could play was 'Seek'.

Phil Gorman has the body of a twenty year old . . . a twenty year old Volvo!

As it happens, he's very conscious of his diet.
Every day he tries to eat something from one of the four main food groups . . .
McDonalds, Burger King, Wimpy and Kentucky Fried Chicken!

Last week, his wife hung out a pair of his Y-Fronts to dry, and a family of New Age Travellers moved in.

He hasn't got a laptop . . .
He hasn't even got a *lap*!

Question: What time is it when Phil Gorman sits on your desk?
Answer: Time to get a new desk.

Being overweight isn't all bad news.
Researchers have discovered a foolproof contraceptive for people that size . . . nudity!

He's a bit depressed at the moment . . . he read the FT this morning and suddenly realised that the Economy is in better shape than *he* is!

PHILOSOPHY

A few years back, I was in a poker tournament which included some of the world's leading players. One of them was the legendary Amarillo Slim, who seemed to me to be more of a cowboy card-specialist than a philosopher.

Wrong.

Amarillo once gave some valuable advice, the wisdom of which transcends mere poker playing. It's equally valid for any business encounter or negotiation.

'Look around the table. If you don't see a sucker, get out of there because the sucker is you!'

Nothing makes it easier to resist temptation than a strong moral upbringing . . . and witnesses.

It doesn't seem to matter how cynical you are, the truth is usually worse.

I'm at a very confused time of life; I don't believe in heaven, I don't believe in hell . . . and I'm beginning to have my doubts about Milton Keynes.

'Wise men talk because they have something to say, fools, because they have to say something.'
Plato said that . . . because he had to say something.

Capitalism without bankruptcy is like Christianity without hell.

Remember: you can pick your friends, and you can pick your nose . . . but you can't pick your friend's nose!

The funny thing about the stock market is that everytime someone buys, someone else sells . . . and they *both* think they're being shrewd.

(Bridging line)

Money isn't everything . . . as a matter of fact, it isn't even enough!

There's nothing like a big broad smile . . . but then of course, there's nothing like a big broad!

He who ties string around fingers, usually remembers to buy yo-yo.

POLITICAL CORRECTITUDE

. . . the natural enemy of subtlety, humour and the English language.

I recently came across a new edition of *Braude's Treasury Of Wit & Humor For All Occasions* in an American bookshop. Underneath the author's name were the words: 'Revisor: Glenn Van Ekeren'.

Once I started thumbing through the book, I realised who Glenn Van Ekeren really was – a Commissar for the Radical Feminist Movement.

He *had* to be.

In his introduction, Van Ekeren boasts that he made language changes where 'gender demarcating' was in question. One consequence of this nonsense is that he describes Norman Brodsky as a 'New York businessperson'.

What the hell's wrong with 'businessman'? Is there any dispute about Norman's gender?

Throughout poor old Jacob's book, extra words were inserted in order not to offend. Every time the word 'he' appeared, it had to be followed by 'and she' or 'or she', regardless of the mess it made of the flow.

Subsituting 'person' for 'woman' or 'man', does nothing for equality or even courtesy. It serves only to diffuse the picture of a character whose description is usually vital when we're setting a scene.

Some years ago, before the feminist movement was hijacked by scary American academics in horrible clothes, they gave us a very useful prefix – 'Ms'. It's an ideal title to use when a lady's marital status is unknown.

The new fanatics, nowadays, would have us lose 'Mr' or 'Mrs' or even 'Ms', and replace them with 'Citizen' or something similar.

I've got news for these nut cases; real women honestly don't need this patronising tosh. They know full well that the word 'mankind' is non-exclusive.
They realise that replacing it with 'humankind' doesn't get rid of the 'man' lurking within.

I hope my lady readers will forgive me for not being too 'gender sensitive'. I'm sure they understand that some lines just won't work for both sexes.

If I had to inject all those extra concessionary words into my one-liners and into the text of this book, the jokes would be far too cumbersome and the narration, unreadable.

I've got enough troubles.

News Flash! Ms Bernadette McButch, the feminist who believes that males and females should at all times be treated absolutely equally, received fatal injuries today . . . trying to milk a bull!

Here's the golden rule – the person who controls the position of the toilet seat, controls the relationship.

Poor girl; she wanted to be a feminist, but her husband wouldn't let her.

Janet Street-Porter argues that, as women comprise fifty-three per cent of the population, there are not nearly enough of them employed in TV.
If it's all about percentage of the population, the BBC should also employ three budgies, two parrots and a mynah bird to read the news!

I've noticed that females hate going through the security machines at airports . . .
I suppose it proves that hell hath no fury like a woman scanned!

I'm sick of women trying to dominate men like they were some kind of domesticated houseboys . . .
To hell with it! I'm a *man*, for God's sake!
Nobody tells *me* how to scrub a floor!

POLITICS AND BUREAUCRACY

John Galsworthy calculated that idealism increases in direct proportion to one's distance from the problem.

It makes a lot of sense when you think about it. For example, I've noticed that most people who favour birth control have already been born . . .

most of those who want to restrict immigration are already here . . .

and the only people wishing to abolish the monarchy are commoners!

But I digress. After all, idealism has no place in a section devoted to the subject of politics.

If you look up 'politics' in the dictionary, it's actually a combination of two words: 'poly' . . . which means 'many', and 'tics . . . which means 'little bloodsuckers'.

The House of Commons is an exclusive and distinguished chamber . . . and we all know what people do in a chamber.

The big question for politicians has always been . . . how do you take money from a taxpayer without disturbing a voter?!

(Bridging line)

Politicians and nappies should be changed often – and for the same reason.

Many people in Britain don't vote at all . . . they feel they can't earn their keep under the Conservatives, and can't keep what they earn under Labour.

(Bridging line)

Mind you, there's one thing both Labour and the Tories have in common – our money!

I think the Government should ask everyone in Britain, whether or not we should have a referendum.

I have come to the conclusion that one useless man is called a disgrace . . . two useless men are called a firm of solicitors . . . and three or more are called . . . the Foreign Office!

Following the lifting of the ten-year public information embargo, it's just been revealed that at the time several foreign nationals were being held prisoner in the Middle East, the Irish SAS were ordered on a secret mission to Beirut.
Unfortunately, they misunderstood their orders, raided Beirut Zoo and released all the ostriches!

It's amazing how many people who run local authorities happen to be authorities on locals . . .

(Bridging line)

Bureaucracy: 'A giant mechanism operated by pygmies.'

(Honoré de Balzac)

In this organization, we know exactly how to welcome visiting government bureaucrats . . . we roll out the red tape.

No wonder most people think Brussels is a joke . . . They're paying one guy in France 500,000 Francs a year, not to plant anything . . . and he's an *undertaker!*

Correguador is the sort of country where 'General Election' means you're only allowed to elect a general.

Old soldiers never die . . . they just go on Sky News and talk bullshit.

April 20th 1889 . . . Adolf Hitler was born.
When he was a toddler and Santa asked him what he wanted for Christmas, little Adolf said, 'Poland!'

The leading government-controlled newspaper in The People's Republic of China is about to run a competition for the best political joke.
First prize is twenty years.

QUIPS AND BITS

We're going to be asking important questions today . . . questions like: 'Will Salman Rushdie ever forgive his ghost writer?'

. . . Questions like: How many dyslexics does it take to light in a screw bulb?

. . . Questions like: When opticians divorce, do they split everything twenty-twenty?

Please don't laugh so long . . . it spoils my timing!

That's my Datapost joke . . . you'll get it in the morning.

Sorry! . . . sometimes when I speak too fast, I say things I haven't even thought of yet!

Finally . . . I always say 'Finally' early on in a speech . . . it gives people hope.

I've got bad news for you . . . that was my best joke!

That's the last time I pinch one of Jimmy Tarbuck's gags!

Ladies and gentlemen, for reasons of safety, please don't try these jokes in your own home!

. . . And now, having tried everything else to impress you, it looks very much like I'm going to have to say something sensible.

(If someone starts to leave during your speech . . .)

Don't tell me, let me guess . . . you're so impressed by my speech you're going out to tell your friends, right?

If you're going for a pizza, I'll have pepperoni and tomatoes.

REPLYING

Some years ago, I made a speech at a prestigious show business dinner at London's Carlton Tower Hotel.

It simply couldn't have gone better.

My material and delivery really hit the spot that night and the room rang with laughter all the way through my piece, for which I was given a standing ovation.

One of my comedy heroes, Barry Cryer, had to follow me. He stood up and said, 'Just before dinner, Mitch and I were having a drink together, and we thought it would be great fun to swap speeches. So here, ladies and gentlemen, is Mitch Murray's speech . . .'

Needless to say, that opening immediately took the game back to Barry, who went on to make a fabulous speech of his own.

What a professional!

Here are some lines you may wish to use in order to thank the person who introduced you, or to acknowledge the previous speaker.

It's always a good idea to anticipate the remarks other speakers are likely to make, and to prepare some appropriate words. Choose well, and they'll sound like brilliant ad libs.

Meanwhile, whether you're a guest, a host, or a hired hand,

feel free to inject one or more of these into the text of your speech.

Thank you, Mr President, for a very flattering introduction . . .
I can see you had no problem reading my handwriting.

May the Lord forgive you for the excess flattery in that introduction, and may he forgive me for enjoying it so much.

I only hope you weren't under oath!

Thank you for that wonderful introduction . . . you've obviously got me confused with somebody else.

If I had any blood left, I'd blush!

A famous American politician once said, 'Praise is like perfume . . . it's all right to smell it as long as you don't swallow it'.
Well, that might be good enough for the humble, but it ain't good enough for me . . . so thanks for the praise – I accept.

Thank you for that wonderful welcome. You've left me speechless . . . I don't know, maybe that's what you had in mind.

Thank you, Mr Chairman, for that wonderful build-down . . .

When you're near the end of a long programme . . .

I'd like to start by thanking the nine previous speakers for whipping this audience into a frenzy of enthusiasm.

As for this evening, I must say I've enjoyed every week of it.

I *was* going to make some financial forecasts tonight, but I've been waiting up here so long, they've all come true!

If I'd known it was going to be like this, I'd have brought something to read!

I must confess, I wasn't really sure what to talk about this evening. I suppose I could have waffled on about nothing very much until it was time for me to sit down and have a brandy, but frankly, I didn't want mine to be just like all the *other* speeches, so instead . . .

Thank you for that lovely dinner . . . I must say it was almost a meal in itself!

Thanking a guest speaker:

I think you'll all agree, ladies and gentlemen, Ed Vickers has proved once again, that he has something in common with the Governor of the Bank of England . . .

All he has to do is speak, and your rate of interest goes up.

(Bridging line)

Tongue-in-cheek lines of thanks:

... but seriously, Ed, your words were very moving ... and, quite frankly, you've made us almost pleased we invited you.

I must say, you really put fire into that speech ... if only you'd put that speech into the fire!

Some speakers are so professional, all you have to do is to put dinner into their mouths, and up comes a speech ...
With Ed Vickers, all you have to do is put a speech into his mouth, and up comes your dinner!

(See also 'Emcee Lines')

RETIREMENT

Ladies and gentlemen, I intend to keep this speech quite short as a courtesy to Stuart Reid. I don't want to keep the poor guy hanging around too long and I'll tell you why ...
When Stuart was young, his heart ruled his head ...
in his middle years, his head ruled his heart ...
now he's sixty-eight and his kidneys rule both!

(Bridging line)

Stuart, when we heard you were about to retire, we passed round the hat to buy you a gift . . .
not only didn't we raise any money . . . but somebody nicked the bloody hat!

The problem with being retired is that your week lacks any shape. It has no real form . . . no misery of Monday mornings, no relief of Friday afternoons, no difference on the weekends.
You never know what day it is, what time it is, where you're supposed to be . . .
Come to think of it, it'll be exactly like you were still working here.

But of course, I happen to know, you've given this company some of the best minutes of your life.

. . . and it's going to be difficult to replace you . . .
mostly because nobody has any idea what you did.

This retirement will make quite a difference to Maggie's life . . . twice as much husband, half as much income.

Ladies and gentlemen, before you leave, I'm sure you'll all be lining up to shake Stuart's hand, but there's really no need . . .
at his age, all you have to do is *hold* his hand and it'll shake all by itself!

A lady director retires . . .

You know, there's an old Chinese proverb . . .

but the one I'm going to dedicate to Mary . . . is from Bolivia:
'One generation plants the trees; another sits and enjoys the benefit   of their shade.'
Here's to you, Mary, for planting those trees.

A few lines for your own retirement . . .

You have no idea, ladies and gentlemen, how wonderful it feels, knowing that forty-five busy people have turned up here this evening just to see me quit. Still, you know what they say, 'give the public what they want' . . .

As you can imagine, for quite some time I've been anticipating my retirement and making plans for the next step, and for the years ahead.

The other day I decided to review my situation. I gained access to my retirement fund . . . shook it . . . unscrewed the lid and emptied it out.

Pathetic, isn't it?

Perhaps now you'll understand the depth of my gratitude . . . not only for twenty-six happy years at Blake's, but also for the free dinner this evening.

Tonight has been a very pleasant way to round off a most rewarding career.
I'm really grateful to all those who organised it and to everybody who came along to share this very special evening with me.

Thank you all.

(See Chapter Five for more material in a retirement speech context.)

RICH AND POOR

Rich? This man gets begging letters from the IMF!

There's something rather disturbing about finding your lawyer's name in the *Sunday Times'* 'Britain's Richest 500'.

(Bridging line)

Last week he went out to buy a couple of golf clubs . . . Wentworth and St Andrews!

(Bridging line)

Recently, he cashed a cheque that was so big . . . the *bank* bounced!

There are three taps on his bathroom basin: 'Hot', 'Cold' and 'Veuve Clicquot'!

(Bridging line)

He made a fortune . . . supplying shoe trees to Imelda Marcos!

I'm now working on my second million . . . I had to give up on my *first* million.

If I died tomorrow, I'd have enough money to live on for the rest of my life!

If you want ugliness, stupidity and failure – don't look at me.
But if you want charisma, brains and wealth . . .
I'll get you someone else!

I'd love to be able to run a Rolls Royce . . .
I *own* a Rolls Royce . . . I just can't afford to run it.

(Bridging line)

I'm not in the *least* worried about my overdraft . . .
Believe me, it's big enough to look after itself.

It's a real pleasure to be standing here, surrounded by the 'crème de la skimmed milk'.

The place is such a dump, they stand Kate Adie in front of it when they want to pretend she's giving live coverage from Beirut!

ROASTS AND INSULTS

The important thing to remember about 'roast' material is that it has to have a ring of truth about it in order to be funny.

These jokes are verbal caricatures. They take a defect or a quirk and exaggerate it.

If, for instance, your Company Secretary is a little – how

can I put it? – unexciting (a fanciful thought, I know, but let's hypothesise), you may well say:

> **Ladies and gentlemen, some people need no introduction . . .**
> **Brian Torrance needs all the introduction he can get. Once seen, never remembered, Brian has that magic ability to light up a room . . . as soon as he *leaves* it. For this man, Valium is a stimulant! . . .**

and so on . . .

But would that material be funny if – despite his profession – Brian Torrance was known to be a hyperactive, colourful dude and the life-and-soul of the party?

Of course not.

The audience laughs at the parody of what it recognises as Brian's insipid disposition. All your roast lines need to have this kind of credibility. The stronger the characteristic, the more effective the routine will be. For instance, if you're going to laugh at his drinking, make sure he drinks for England and is not just a 'white wine with a meal' man.

But wait! Don't let's go overboard with this 'truth' stuff.

Audience *perception* takes priority over truth.

Let's say a guy in the office, perhaps because of his shyness, has an undeserved reputation as an intellectual lightweight. Even though you happen to know that he's really very bright indeed, you must make jokes on the basis of the way people *see* him rather than focus your humour on the true situation as only you know it.

If you can't stomach making yourself party to a misconception of this kind, don't joke about him at all.

Whatever you do, never contrive a situation or a characteristic in order to justify using a one-liner, no matter how funny you think it is.

Try to hit the button, but don't be too cruel. Even if the roastee is liable to take it well, many members of the audience are going to be concerned for your victim's feelings if you cross that sensitive line.

Think about the person you wish to rib; you may find something in his (never her) appearance – shortish, big nose, beer belly?

Is he an insensitive yob? A mummy's boy? A dirty old man?

I hope so. All that makes for a much better speech.

The ideal subject for a roast is an equal. Someone of exactly the same status.

Earlier on in the book, under a section entitled 'The Boss', I've explained how much care you should take when 'roasting' important customers or people of higher rank.

Making jokes at the expense of underlings should be treated with as much care and trepidation as you would apply when cracking gags about superiors.

Don't bully, don't humiliate. The victim won't find it funny and the audience will cringe.

There's another reason to be gentle with your subordinate. One day that spotty little sod may be promoted above you in the company hierarchy and overnight you may find yourself up a quaintly named creek without any means of propulsion.

It simply ain't worth it.

Another difficult situation arises when you don't know your victim too well. The audience will not grant you the right to make fun of a virtual stranger. Under these circumstances, even words of mild mockery will sound highly insulting.

It may well be worth cultivating a brief friendly contact with the subject before the speech is made, in order to validate your banter. You may even ask your victim if he objects to your poking fun at him. (Don't worry, they *never* object.) This gives you the chance to create the illusion of prior acquaintanceship when you set up your one-liners . . .

Earlier on, I was chatting to your Vice President, Alex Randle, and apparently he's rather anxious that no one should make a fuss over him tonight . . . he asks that you treat him only as you would any other great British industrialist . . .

You see? You've given yourself just enough 'speech cred' to be able to go at him.

We've now identified three problem areas:
- Roasting superiors.
- Roasting inferiors.
- Roasting people you don't know very well.

Time, therefore, for me to introduce my latest fiendish technique: a device designed to give you the benefit of the jokes whilst shielding you from too much responsibility.

But first, a small ceremony . . .

I name this schtick; 'SAFE SLANDER'.
May God bless it, and all who assail with it.

The idea of 'Safe Slander' is to attack the ugly things people say about the subject of your roast. You appear to defend the victim and side with him in outrage.

This way, although you distance yourself from the sentiment, you still pick up all the laughs.

> **People say he has a personality problem. I don't know what they're talking about . . .**
> **Who started the rumour that when he was in Canada, a load of baby seals got together and clubbed *him*!?**

> **How stupid ! . . .**
> **Why do people spread these silly stories?**

> **They say he climbed a mountain in Switzerland, called out 'Hello!', and the echo said, 'Jump!'**

> **It's not true, it's not nice, it's not fair!**

You may even mildly rebuke the audience for dignifying these scandalous rumours with laughter.

> **Why are you laughing? We're talking about a man's reputation here!**

Do you think it's funny?! Do you think it's right that people should say he's the only man in history ever to be told by Mother Theresa to 'Piss off!'?

Give the guy a break.

(Make sure you follow this routine with a smile; we don't want to confuse anybody.)

One more thing about roasts; make absolutely certain that none of the lines you're using against your victims apply equally to you.

If the Post Office recently gave your nose its own postcode, don't bother to make cracks about someone with a big schnozz.

If you're so thin that Steve Davis keeps chalking your head, don't try to roast that skinny guy in Credit Control.

If your teeth protrude so much that when you smile, you comb your beard, don't waste your time joking about the General Manager's overbite!

Hey . . . I've just pictured you.

Urghhh!

Okay, it's finally time to go a-one-lining.

These are nearly all general ('flexi') roast lines and are easily adaptable, but do make sure your subject is emotionally equipped to be able to put up with a put-down.

Don't worry, I'm not going to make fun of Pete Martin . . . I can't stand people who make fun of someone just because they're bloody useless!

It's impossible to praise this guy too highly.
In fact it's impossible to praise him at all . . . he's crap!

His talent is second to none . . . Wally Nunn of Sidcup.

Last time we met he insulted me . . . it was very hurtful. He said I was lying when I called him a prick!

For any of you who doubt the high regard in which Peter Martin is held in the business world, I think I only need tell you that this is the man of whom Sir John Harvey-Jones once said, 'Please don't mention his name again, I've got a split lip!'

But he's nobody's fool, and that's a great pity because, there's nothing more sad than a lonely fool.

In our industry, Pete Martin is considered to be a veritable farce . . . er . . . force!

Around the office, this man is God! . . . He's rarely seen, he's holier than thou and if he does anything it's considered a bloody miracle!

He's very considerate to his inferiors. He can afford to be . . . there's so *few* of them.

He's one of the finest industrialists of the day . . . bloody lousy at night, but . . . wonderful during the day.

Unfettered by self-righteous ethics, rigid planning, over-emphasis on efficiency . . . unhindered by skill or technique, this man is *above* professionalism. He is in a category of his own . . . crap!

What can one really say about Pete Martin?
Anyone who says he's unimaginative . . . has obviously seen his latest business plan.

Right at the very beginning of his time with the firm, Pete Martin showed himself to have exceptional talents . . .
however, it wasn't long before he outgrew this phase and . . .
now Pete has developed into a man who has a fundamental understanding of what big business is really all about.
Mind you, he certainly doesn't seem to allow that to affect his judgement.

In this industry, he's regarded as Nobility . . .
He has no 'bility at all!

He's a highly responsible executive . . .
he's responsible for lower profits, he's responsible for inefficiency, he's responsible for bad publicity . . .

A recent study showed that if his new business strategy recommendations were stacked up in a single pile . . .
they'd be much easier to feed into the shredder.

Nobody thinks more highly of him than I do and that means he's got a problem 'cos I think he's a prat!

He'd be the first to tell you he's got no real talent . . . and I'd be the second.

He's a man of many parts . . . but then, of course, so was Frankenstein.

You know there's something very funny about Pete . . . he still complains that the doctor slapped his bottom before he was old enough to enjoy it.

But please don't underestimate Pete Martin's contribution to the success of this company . . .
I want to be the one to do that.

He's a man of hidden talents . . . well there's certainly no sign of any so far.

You all know the song, 'To know him is to love him' . . . Pete Martin has heard that song as well!

When the doctor announced 'It's a boy!', his father took one look at the kid and asked for a second opinion.

This man knows exactly where he's going, and where he's been . . . he just doesn't know where he is!

All in all, Pete Martin is a difficult man to forget . . . but well worth the effort!

(Many of these one-liners are interchangeable with those under 'Emcee Lines'.)

SALES AND THOSE WHO MAKE 'EM

Those of you who sell, or administer sales personnel, are currently doing so in a context of heightened consumer-awareness. These days, your customers are well informed, mindful of their options and able to exercise their rights more vigorously than ever before . . .

In other words . . . smart arses!

Let's face it, the old sales clichés won't work anymore . . . what you need are *new* clichés . . .

Don't look at me, I don't cleesh.

The first rule of sales management is never to talk down to your sales team . . . but I'm sure most of you wouldn't understand that.

This year, we have a new sales incentive scheme . . . Whoever sells the most keeps his job.

A sales team is something you have to work at, nurture, add to . . . you know, like a compost heap!

(Flexi line)

Sales personnel are employed mainly to say things their employer wouldn't dare put into print.

What a salesman! . . . this guy could sell Salman Rushdie a timeshare in Teheran!

What a salesman! . . . this guy could have talked Adam into eating another apple!

What a salesman! . . . this guy could sell a padded bra to Anna-Nicole Smith!

What a salesman! . . . this guy could sell nail polish to the Venus de Milo!
(He could certainly do no worse than that arms dealer.)

What a salesman! . . . this guy could sell an egg-beater to Humpty Dumpty's widow!

Commission is a little bit like sex . . . you're always hoping for more than you get.

(Sing to the tune of 'Tradition')

. . . Commisshu-u-u-n, Commishun!

Waiting for him to close a deal is like leaving a light burning in the window for Lord Lucan!
He owes a lot of his success to good contacts . . . which is suprising, 'cos every time he sneezes, they fly out of his eyes!

On his very first day as a salesman he got two orders . . . 'Get out!' and 'Stay out!'

SMOKING

There's a new support group – 'Nicotine Anonymous'. When you feel a craving for a cigarette, you call up another member of the group, he comes over and you get pissed together!

(Bridging line)

I've been smoking thirty a day since I was sixteen years old, and I can assure you, there's nothing wrong with *my* lung!

I think it's a bloody liberty the way smokers are treated. Why *should* I have to step outside just to have a smoke? . . . I don't care *what* the pilot says!

(Bridging line)

He looked very distinguished, standing there with a pipe in his mouth . . . but then he started blowing bubbles.

Here's some good news for Lenny Ross . . . Lenny, your Uncle Barney has finally stopped smoking.
That message just came through from the boys at Golders Green Crematorium.

I stopped smoking cold turkey . . . *and* cigarettes, both on the same day.

According to my own personal survey, more people die of boredom listening to experts going on about smoking, than are ever killed by tobacco!

SPIVS

Some people are, by nature, naturally upright, honest and others are downright dishonest. This section is dedicated to them.

If asked – and I haven't been – I would describe a spiv as someone with a little less devotion to honesty than the law actually requires. Someone who's credibility has developed stretch marks.

Most of these lines are actionable. They're only here for you to look at – don't ever use them.

If you do, tell the judge you saw them in Bob Monkhouse's book.

In our industry, this man is an icon . . . *icon*!
. . . in fact, that's his motto.

At the moment, he's spending a year in a tax shelter . . .
Ford *Open* tax shelter.

Later on, we're going to hold a free draw. First prize is
£50 . . .
second prize is Harry Fisher's cheque for £300!

They say seeing is believing . . . well, I've been seeing
Harry Fisher for years and I *still* don't believe him!

His contracts were religiously drafted . . . the big print
giveth and the small print taketh away!

He trains his staff always to remember that, okay,
honesty is the best policy yeah? But it's not necessarily
the *only* policy.

(That's just to prove I know how to speak Estuary English.)

He's a flexible man . . . he's willing to bend the facts
and stretch the truth!

Last year his tax return won a Pulitzer Prize for fiction.

He's a man of convictions . . . admittedly, most of
them were overturned on appeal!

He assured me he'd invest my money as if it were his
own, and pretty soon . . . it was!

But he's a sentimental old softie really . . .
he's still got the first fiver he ever embezzled.

He's in hospital, at the moment, for a serious operation
. . . a triple-conscience by-pass.

He's following in his father's fingerprints.

He seems too good to be true . . . he isn't.

He tries to live up to his ideals . . . which is why he walks with a stoop.

He's got that brilliant knack of being able to sell things he doesn't have, to people who don't want 'em!

He's formed himself into a Limited Credibility Company.

Even his *cash* bounces!

There are only two things I don't like about him . . . his face!

This is a man who's followed the Ten Commandments all through his life, but never quite managed to catch up with any of them.

He has all the sincerity of Bernard Matthews saying to a turkey . . . 'Trust me!'

Say what you like, he's in great demand . . . in fact there are three big companies after him at the moment – the Gas Company, the Phone Company and the Electric Company!

This guy is doing the work of two men . . . the Kray twins!

When he first started out in the business, he couldn't get arrested. Since then his luck has changed.

But he's an honest man . . . he's as honest as the day is . . . oh my God, is that the time!?

(Bridge into closing)

(See also 'Bad Payers' and 'Bastards')

STATISTICS

Statistics are like ladies of the night. Once you get them down, you can do anything with them.

(Mark Twain)

Four thousand statisticians are due to converge in Geneva next year for an international convention . . . Think of it, four thousand statisticians all in one place . . . what are the chances of that?

Torture numbers, and they'll confess to anything.

Local government statistics show that the average ratepayer produces 926 kilos of rubbish a year . . . Of course, it's a much higher figure for local government statisticians.

(Flexi line)

According to a recent AA survey, one out of every four tyres is unbalanced . . . even worse, so is one out of every four drivers!

(Bridging line)

Statistics can be used to support anything . . . including statisticians.

The government has just conducted a £30 million survey, and they've found out that three out of four people in this country represent seventy five per cent of the population.

Nine out of ten doctors surveyed said you shouldn't pay any attention to the other eight.

(Bridging line)

Statistics are like witnesses . . . they'll testify for either side.

Statistics prove that more accidents happen in the home than anywhere else, so drink up! –
What d'you want to go back there for?

(Bridging line)

STRESS

Well, it's been a rubber-hose-up-the-exhaust-pipe kinda day.

Stressed out? You *could* say that . . . he's the only guy I know with clenched *hair*!

Stressed out? You *could* say that . . . this poor guy once played Russian Roulette . . . with a catapult!

Swear box? In our office? You're kidding . . . we use a skip!

I think I must be suffering from varicose brains.

I admit it . . . I've often contemplated suicide . . . not my own, mind you.

My doctor said I've got to give up wine, women and reading the FT.

(Bridging line)

I've decided . . . from now on I'm going to learn to relax, even if I have to work at it twenty-four hours a day, seven days a week!

STUPID/NAÏVE

A: I sometimes wonder about Simon's judgement.
B: What makes you say that?
A: He invested heavily in the BCCI.
B: So what? Lots of people invested in the BCCI.
A: Last week?

This guy is several Air Miles short of a trip to Paris.

Talk about thick! Once, during a power cut at Leicester Square Station, he was stuck on an escalator for four hours.
I asked him, 'Why didn't you just walk down?' . . .
He said, 'I was on my way up!'

He once built a ship in a bottle.
We had to break the bottle to get him out!

When it comes to business matters, he has a sixth sense . . .
Shame the other five are missing!

He's at his wits' end. It was a very short journey.

He never quite understood the difference between arson and incest . . . in 1981, he set fire to his sister!

I told him straight . . . I told him he had a minuscule command of the English language, pathetic communication skills and that he seemed to be completely oblivious to what was going on around him . . .
Quick as a flash, back came his reply . . . 'Do what?'

He's a little naïve when it comes to sexual matters . . .
He actually believes that 'mutual climax' is an insurance company in Omaha!

He thinks Price Waterhouse is a 'pay toilet'.

He thinks Dun and Bradstreet is an intersection!

He's a man of hidden shallows.

He knows nothing of current affairs; he thinks Slobodan Milosevic is one of the Flowerpot Men!

Soixante-neuf? What would *I* want with sixty eggs?!

I'll never forget the secretary we had in our Dublin office; every time the little bell sounded on her typewriter, she broke for tea.

SUPPLIERS

They can certainly charge. At first I wasn't sure whether what they sent me was an invoice or a ransom note!

The worst thing you can hear from a builder is 'Uh-oh . . .
The 'Uh' is four grand and the 'oh' is another fifteen hundred.

The charge they made for servicing my car was ridiculous . . . £500 to tune the engine!
Who did they use? Sir Michael Bloody Tippett!?

TAX

The City is very tough these days. If you do something wrong you get fined, if you do something right you get taxed.

My local Inland Revenue office has two signs over the door – the one going in says: 'Watch Your Step' and the one going out says: 'Watch Your Language'.

There are only two certainties – death and taxes . . . unfortunately, they don't come along in that order.

Isn't it about time the Revenue started giving Air Miles?

If business gets any worse, I won't have to lie about my income any more.

I've always tried to pay my taxes with a smile . . . unfortunately, the Revenue prefers cash!

There are only two kinds of people who whinge about their income tax – men and women.

Harry Fisher has untold wealth . . . at least it's untold as far as the Inland Revenue's concerned.

After the Chancellor has taken enough to balance the budget, you and I have to try to budget the balance.

Isn't the Inland Revenue's head office in Andover?

The best things in life are free . . . plus VAT.

Is Blackpool Tower merely St Paul's Cathedral after tax has been deducted?

**. . . and now a toast – to Her Majesty's Inland Revenue
. . . you've really got to hand it to them!**

TECHNOLOGY AND COMMUNICATIONS

In recent years, many large companies appear to have started using special roulette wheels which are designed to spin once for every incoming call. You are the ball, and the grooves are marked: 'He's in a meeting', 'Bear with me for a moment', 'Our computer's down', 'Sorry, I'm going to have to put you on hold' and thirty-two other excuses, clichés and annoyances.

Other firms take the trouble to train their switchboard staff instantly to assess the relative nuisance value of the caller and to allocate the appropriate 'Music On Hold' selection.

Someone calling in to chase non-payment of an invoice, for instance, will score much higher than a day-to-day enquiry and will therefore have to listen to the Andy McTavish Bagpipe Ensemble. The idea being, of course, that within eight bars maximum, his or her patience will run out and the invoice chaser will hang up.

Who wouldn't?

Believe me, even Andy McTavish's *mother* would slam the receiver down after a chorus of that crap.

A Grade 'B' nuisance call – a good customer with a valid complaint – will cop for East Anglian folk music, punctuated with reassuring words like: 'Please stay on the line until the next operator gets back from maternity leave'. However, a potential sale, if placed on hold at all, will be able to enjoy Frank Sinatra, Whitney Houston or one of *my* songs.

Oh dear, this theory is beginning to crumble.

Let's hear the lines . . .

> Back in 1853, they invented the bath-tub.
> Then, in 1878, the first switchboard telephone service
> began . . .
> What luxury!
> What a window of opportunity!
> You could have sat in the bath for twenty-five years
> without having to get out of it to answer the
> 'phone!

> Why do car 'phones always ring just as you drive into
> the car-wash?

> The giant NASA Radio Telescope that is scanning the
> universe searching for intelligent life, picked up Stan
> Pearce on his mobile 'phone.
> Never mind NASA, keep searching.

> How does he expect people to take him seriously!
> . . . His mobile 'phone is made by *Fisher-Price*, for
> God's sake!

> They've set up a new 0891 number you can call to test
> your IQ. It costs five pounds a reading and the way it
> works is . . . if you stay on the line for over a minute,
> you're a moron!

> If you want to drive somebody nuts, just send them a
> fax saying: 'Imperative you ignore previous fax'.

My assistant's a little accident-prone ... last week, he got his tie caught in the fax machine and ended up in Liverpool!

I've got so used to fax machines, I can't read anything unless it's curled up!

'The factory of the future will have only two employees – a man and a dog.
The man will be there to feed the dog.
The dog will be there to keep the man from touching the equipment.'

(Warren Bennis)

Japanese motor manufacturers are employing something that does the work of five men ... a programmable robot.
The British also employ something that does the work of five men ... ten men!

I think Marconi must have been a little feeble-minded ... fancy inventing radio when there weren't even any programmes.

To some people, electronics is big business ...
to Birds Eye, micro-chips are small potatoes.

As you know, all modern products are guaranteed. Of course, with some manufacturers, if anything goes wrong, that immediately invalidates the guarantee ...

July the 31st, marks the discovery of Oxygen by Carl Wilhelm Scheele in 1774.
Up until then, people used to breathe in any old crap.

THE TRIBUTE

Every now and then you may be called upon to shower praise upon a colleague or associate. He or she may be retiring, receiving an award, moving in, moving up, moving on, or even being buried. From an early age, we British are urged to keep a stiff upper lip. By implication, therefore, we're allowed to let the lower one go limp.

Is it any wonder that some of us have trouble being understood?

More to the point, unlike our American cousins, we are not very comfortable using gushing, extravagant language when praising individuals. That's our problem; our inhibitions and hang-ups are often liable to endanger the expression of our genuine feelings.

In short, sometimes sincerity just doesn't ring true.

We all know many genuine people who simply can't help sounding like phonies; it's the language they use and the tone they adopt.

In a tribute speech, it can be quite difficult to maintain the balance between flowery, sentimental cornball and cold formality. You need to let your audience know how much you admire the subject of your speech, yet, if you overdo the superlatives, the crowd is liable to start throwing up en masse.

There are other considerations.

If you're a manager paying tribute to one of your staff, you'll want to avoid any charge of favouritism. You can't risk downgrading the rest of the team by implication. And remember, the human body is strange . . . occasionally, too much patting on the back will result in a swollen head!

All in all, a tribute speech has to be a fine balancing trick.

Make sure you avoid being too nice for too long. Alternate your sincere observations with little bits of humour.

I call this style – 'The Ping Pong Principle'.

The 'Ping Pong Principle' works like this:

- You praise . . . you sting.

- You acclaim . . . you knock.

- You toast . . . you roast.

For example, here's a lighthearted 'softener' you could use in order to break up the monotony of continuous praise. Insert the line either exactly as it is, or adapt it to the world of sport, politics, or voluntary work:

> **As if all these achievements weren't enough, in his lifetime this man has also made a major contribution to the St. John Ambulance Brigade . . . he stayed *out* of it.**
>
> (Flexi line)

From here, swiftly move back to positive humour:

**But we're lucky to have him . . . he's brilliant!
His IQ is higher than Ian Paisley's blood pressure.**

Ping! Break again:

**Yes, Bill Huntley is a great organiser, he's warm, he's
intelligent, he's . . .
Sorry Bill, I can't read your writing, what does that
say? . . .
Oh yes . . . 'modest'.**

Pong! – Back to positive humour:

**A lot of people are surprised that Bill is a friend of
Cabinet Ministers, top entertainers, royalty . . . but
why not? Even *they* need someone to look up to.**

. . . and so on.

Here are a few more 'positive' lines:

**This man is such a wonderful, saintly, honest person,
that when he goes to church, the priest confesses to
him!**

**He's a corporate strategist, an accountant, he was an
athlete, he's been a writer . . . and on the seventh day,
he rested.**

This man could charm the knickers off a transvestite!

As far as anyone can tell, he hasn't got a single redeeming vice.

His charisma surpasses even my own.

He has more talent in his little finger than . . . in any of his other fingers . . . but what he does in his private life is not our concern today.

Merely to call him a businessman, is like calling Michelangelo a decorator.

You'll find several usable examples of 'positive' humour in other sections of this book. Look for the jokes which portray your subject as he or she would wish to be seen.

Your customer may like to be thought of as powerful, your boss could be proud of his wealthy life-style, perhaps 'super-chic' is the image your young PA favours for herself . . .

The lines are all here. Choose them and use them. Take the trouble. It's worth it.

Hopefully, your speech will be received and remembered, not merely as lip-service, but as a warm and genuine tribute of admiration and respect.

WOMANISERS AND OTHER INCORRIGIBLES

Duncan Bradley can't be with us tonight; he's had to satisfy demands from abroad . . .
this time, the broad is a Mrs Doris Appleyard from Leicester.

Duncan started going out with girls fairly late in life
. . . about two years into his marriage!

He celebrated his Silver Wedding with a romantic
dinner for two at the Waterside Inn . . .
His wife just stayed in and watched TV.

They were divorced because of arithmetic . . . she put
two and two together.

Duncan has always had an eye for a pretty girl . . . but
it isn't his *eye* that gets him into trouble . . . at least
he always keeps *that* in its own socket!

This is the man who joined a woman to forget the
Foreign Legion!

His last girlfriend had a beautiful face, a superb figure
and took only fourteen minutes to inflate . . .

Of course there were problems from time to time, but
he always managed to patch things up.

His motto is: 'If at first you don't succeed . . . try her
with another Vodka and Bitter Lemon.'

You know, everything Richard Branson touches turns
to gold . . .
Everything Duncan Bradley touches screams for help.

He's a pretty flash guy . . . in fact, he's been arrested
for it.

He was the original corporate flasher . . . he used to throw open his raincoat and show his CV.

He's been exposing himself in the park for almost a decade.
The question is, should he retire . . . or stick it out for another year?

He knows everything there is to know about wine . . . this is the man who jumped on the girl who jumped on the grapes!

> (Bridging line)

He likes to do magic . . . last Christmas, he disappeared with that pretty little girl in Accounts.

She asked him, 'Why are you undressing me with your eyes?'
He answered, 'Because I've got arthritis in my hands.'

> (Bridging line)

He loved her for her mind . . . until he found out that sex was the furthest thing from it.

Every woman looks alike to him . . . worth one.

It'll be hard for somebody to fill his shoes . . . especially since half the time he can't remember where he left 'em!

I've no idea what to get him for his birthday . . . what do you get for the man who's had everybody?

WOMEN IN BUSINESS

Some men find it difficult to see the female executive as anything more than a typist made good.

On countless occasions, I've watched women bite their tongues in the face of crass, patronising comments from thoughtless male colleagues.

I've witnessed almost palpable restraint from these females who often happen to be twice as good as their tormentors.

I've admired their self-control and, at the same time, been highly embarrasssed by the behaviour of members of my own sex.

In my experience, not only are women in business more focused than most men, they also manage to get more enjoyment out of their work.

And if you think I'm creeping, you're absolutely right.

As a woman, not only do you have to convince an audience of your excellence at what you do, you also have to appear confident yet not strident, good-humoured yet not bitchy, feminine yet one of the boys, a good sport yet no pushover.

Sister, I don't envy you.

All through this book, I've warned men not to make jokes about women. Women, on the other hand, are perfectly at liberty to say whatever they wish about men. This will not be regarded as sexist.

I've no idea why not, but there we are.

Let's start with a smattering of anti-man lines:

I may like the simple things in life, but that doesn't mean I'd want to *work* for one of them.

There are three types of men in business today . . . the creative, the dedicated and the majority.

Statistics show there are three ages when men misbehave . . . young, old and middle.

As Mae West said, 'Give a man a free hand and he'll run it all over you!'

Some husbands come in handy around the house . . . others come in unexpectedly!

The real reason a dog is a man's best friend is that the dog doesn't understand a word he's saying.

Husbands are like fires. They go out when unattended.
(Zsa Zsa Gabor)

I nearly didn't make it tonight . . . I was trying to catch up with my mail . . .
Never mind, I'll nail him tomorrow.

A woman's natural use of language, indeed her entire approach, is quite different from that of a man.

When it comes to making speeches, she should be aware that certain gags and quips may sound somewhat incompatible with the feminine image. A woman has to select her lines and choose her words with a subtle, delicate touch. It's not at all easy, but when she does get it right, there's nothing funnier.

My favourite comic happens to be a woman – Joan Rivers.

Joan often flirts with bad taste jokes and lavatorial humour, but I forgive her. I forgive her because most of the time, her one-liners are as good as one-liners ever get:

'Nancy Reagan's skin is so tight, when she crosses her legs her mouth snaps open!'

That's more than a one-liner, it's a *movie!*
Coming from another woman, it's even more effective.

One day, perhaps, I'll write a book of one-liners for women. Until then, ma'am, you're on your own.

Not every man can handle being married to a strong-minded, determined, high achiever. The husband of such a woman has to be very secure and laid back. Personally, I think Denis Thatcher got it right . . . he once told a curious reporter that, not only did he wear the pants in his family, he also washed and ironed them.

These days more ladies than ever before, are involved in successful careers of their own. In many households, the female head of the family is just as likely to be away from home as is the male.

Of course, years ago, marriage was very much like the Oscar ceremony; on a Friday night, the wife would step forward and say, 'May I have the envelope, please?'

Times have changed.

Here's something for the ultra-busy bee:

> **The other night, my husband said, 'Carole, you're completely at home in so many fields; you're at home in local government, you're at home in the business world, you're at home in charity work . . . in fact, you're at home in everything but home'.**

> **Well, I have to admit, our social life has been suffering quite a bit. Nowadays my *back* goes out more than I do . . . but I'm sure all that'll change once the season is over.**

Here's an opener for one of those occasions when your role is that of the honouree's spouse . . .

> **If I'd only known before I started getting involved with Nigel, that one day, I was going to have to stand up in public and make a speech, believe me, I'd never have answered his advert in Private Eye!**

X-TRA STUFF

> **The early Nineties witnessed a tremendous growth in small businesses. Lots of people became small businesses . . . for instance, most of the large businesses!**

> **The recession was so catastrophic, that not only did lots of men go bankrupt, some of them even went back to their wives.**

Even the people who never used to pay, stopped buying.

My pal Enzo recently had to close down one of his hairdressing shops because he just couldn't manage to make split ends meet.

Recessions don't worry me, I was a failure during the boom.

Sign on a closed-down store: 'We undersold John Lewis'.

A business needs 'downsizing' when rumours of 'downsizing' take a week to go from one end of the office to the other.

The secret of management is to keep the guys who hate you away from the guys who are still undecided!

They say he's the very best in his own field . . .
I wish I could afford *my* own field . . . I have to make do with a crummy back garden.

I once climbed a mountain and asked a wise man in a cave . . .
'What's the secret of financial success?'
He said, 'If I knew that, do you really think I'd be buggering about up here in a bloody cave?'

The major airlines have announced that from now on, instead of cutting fares, they're going to fly you twenty-five per cent further than you want to go.

What ever happened to young, presentable air hostesses?
Last time I flew with an American airline, the cabin crew looked like they used to work for Orville and Wilbur!

Air fares have been increasing. Even the cost of going up is going up . . . unless you're Hugh Grant where the reverse applies.

The town of Kiloony on the South-West coast of Ireland recently saw the arrival of its first escalator. During the department store's opening ceremony, the mayor suddenly screamed out, 'For God's sake turn it off or you'll have a basement full of stairs!'

Do you realise that if there weren't any gays, Harrods would be self-service?!

A man lay dying in his flat when there was a knock on the door.
'Who's there?', called the dying man.
'The angel of death', replied the solemn visitor.
'Thank goodness, I thought it was an insurance salesman!'

What an interesting economy . . . BHP is down to 21 and Dolly Parton is up to 44!

When he bought a vase in the antique shop, he thought he was getting Ming . . . but he only got stung!

She walked into a dress shop in Finchley and asked the manager, 'Is it all right if I try on that blue dress in the window?' . . .
The manager said, 'Go right ahead – it might help business!'

The showroom was so crowded, my braces broke, and it was fifteen minutes before my trousers fell down!

Life in the fast lane is very stressful . . . especially in a Skoda.

Chapter Fifteen

CLOSING MESSAGE

It's amazing how the function of writing a book concentrates and organises one's mind, to the extent that the author improves his own grip on the subject.

In other words, by arranging and articulating my ideas into book form, I've been polishing up my own operating methods.

You, the reader, probably think I've given away all my best systems and techniques, but I'm now vastly more accomplished here at the end of my book than I was at the beginning, so I'm still way ahead of you.

Bloody discouraging, isn't it?

Before I wrap this sucker up, let's get something straight; as author of this book, I bear an awesome burden.

You may be Chairman of the Board, CEO, Company Secretary or Middle Management.

Alternatively, you could be at the very beginning of your career in a job so lousy that getting fired is one of the *perks*.

Or perhaps you're self-employed. In that case, you're probably working for the most ruthless boss of all.

While you're out there in the dog-eat-dog world of commerce, having to keep an eye on your jealous colleagues, having to humour your boss, having to please your clients and, at the same time, trying to reconcile all of this with a normal family life – spare a thought for me.

Here *I* am, sitting in the sunshine of Tahiti, tapping out pearls of wisdom on my laptop and sipping my Banana Daquiri.

Now, to the untrained eye, it may *appear* that I have a better job. But consider this . . .

On March 28th 1775, the American revolutionary, Patrick Henry, made his famous speech, ending with the impassioned words – 'Give me liberty or give me death!'

Just before they hanged him, he cancelled his speechwriter's Christmas bonus.

A little harsh, but understandable.

Speechwriting, as my story illustrates, is an astonishing responsibility, and one speech can really make a difference – it certainly changed Patrick's life.

Well, it sort of ended it really.

In your case, although the stakes may not be quite as high, the balance of the image you present is critical: it directly relates to two factors – where you are in the company, and where you want to be.

The material you use should at all times be appropriate to your position in the firm, yet, at the same time, it should hint at your potential to those who matter.

Your challenge is to find that small amount of territory between timidity and over-confidence and to live there for the duration of your speech.

Your judgement in selecting material from the wide variety on offer in the preceding pages will be crucial, so be very careful.

Remember, you only have to add an 's' to laughter and it's *slaughter*!

Remember what happened to Gerald Ratner, all because of one little throwaway line in which he described his merchandise as 'crap'.

People just don't appreciate the old British understatement any more, do they?

One more thing.

If you bought this book in an effort to improve your position in your firm – no problem – that's one of the things it was designed to do. However, if you're already at, or near the top, you should immediately go back to the bookshop, buy as many of these books as you can, and destroy them before those hungry, ambitious sons of bitches farther down the ladder learn too much and start snapping at your heels.

As Tarzan said to Jane when he came home exhausted one night; 'It's a bloody jungle out there!'

Mitch Murray

INDEX OF KEY WORDS

This list is by no means comprehensive. You may still have to do a considerable amount of detective work in order to find just the line you're looking for. Furthermore, although your key word may direct you to a section, for example 'Cheat – *see* Spivs, Womanisers', there may well be many more lines relevant to cheats in other sections like 'Bad Payers' or 'Bastards' .

Hey. At least I'm giving you credit for some intelligence.

Enjoy the search.